Coasters, Etc. 2e

An Integrated Office Simulation

Maureen L. Margolies

Professor

Raymond Walters College

University of Cincinnati

Cincinnati, Ohio

D1450696

THOMSON

SOUTH-WESTERN

Australia · Brazil · Canada · Mexico · Singapore · Spain · United Kingdom · United States

Coasters, Etc., An Integrated Office Simulation, 2ⁿᵈ edition
Maureen L. Margolies

VP/Editorial Director
Jack W. Calhoun

VP/Editor-in-Chief
Karen Schmohe

Acquisitions Editor
Jane Congdon

Project Manager
Dr. Inell Bolls

Production Manager
Patricia Matthews Boies

Production Editor
Colleen A. Farmer

VP/Director of Marketing
Carol Volz

Marketing Manager
Mike Cloran

Marketing Coordinator
Georgianna Wright

Manufacturing Coordinator
Charlene Taylor

Art Director
Tippy McIntosh

Compositor
settingPace, LLC

Cover and Internal Designer
Lou Ann Thesing

Cover Photo Source
Lester Lefkowitz

Printer
Banta Company

ASIA (including India)
Thomson Learning
5 Shenton Way
#01-01 UIC Building
Singapore 068808

CANADA
Thomson Nelson
1120 Birchmount Road
Toronto, Ontario
Canada M1K 5G4

AUSTRALIA/NEW ZEALAND
Thomson Learning Australia
102 Dodds Street
Southbank, Victoria 3006
Australia

UK/EUROPE/MIDDLE EAST/AFRICA
Thomson Learning
High Holborn House
50-51 Bedford Road
London WC1R 4LR
United Kingdom

LATIN AMERICA
Thomson Learning
Seneca, 53
Colonia Polanco
11560 Mexico
D.F., Mexico

SPAIN (includes Portugal)
Thomson Paraninfo
Calle Magallanes, 25
28015 Madrid, Spain

Contents

Introduction

Coasters, Etc. contains five projects, each providing typical work performed by an entry-level administrative assistant in a real job situation. The projects simulate sales support activities for the Group Sales Division of an amusement park. The tasks are based on actual job situations that utilize the skills necessary to work in a computerized office.

This office simulation is intended for use with a variety of business application software including word processing, spreadsheet, database, desktop publishing, and presentation graphics. In addition, students have the option of using electronic calendaring, e-mail, facsimile, and the Internet to further simulate the telecommunications features of the offices of the Twenty-First Century. *Coasters, Etc.* is designed for students who have basic software and computer knowledge, but may also be used as a capstone course for students studying information processing.

Features

The simulation is organized by project. Each project simulates the tasks to be completed in about a week. Some tasks will take more than a week to complete. Students use critical thinking skills to determine what tasks will be completed and the order of completion. To obtain directions they will use e-mail messages (on the student CD-ROM), "Notes from Melinda," and their own "To Do" lists along with source documents to complete the tasks. Template files for selected tasks are also included on the student CD. Each project includes a Project Plan form for organizing the work and a Project Evaluation form used to analyze their work and time management skills.

Acknowledgments

Special thanks to Karen Bean, Blinn College, Information Management, Brenham, Texas, for her input in the revision of this product.

Objectives

As students complete each project, the following objectives should be met:

1. Create a work environment in a simulated setting that is both interesting and challenging.
2. Develop organization skills through the planning and prioritizing of tasks in each project.
3. Instill a proactive approach to working by studying the tasks that need to be completed and the best way to get the job done.
4. Develop problem-solving skills by working through directions on specific tasks the first time and following up on similar tasks using previous experience.
5. Use critical thinking skills to analyze, prioritize, develop, write, and create business documents.
6. Use current technology available in business and communications software to work efficiently and effectively.
7. Develop research skills to acquire and distribute information effectively.
8. Understand the role and responsibilities of an administrative assistant in the business world.

Coasters, Etc. contains five projects, each providing typical work performed by an entry-level administrative assistant in a real job situation. The projects simulate sales support activities for the Group Sales Division of an amusement park. The tasks are based on actual job situations that utilize the skills necessary to work in a computerized office.

Organization of the Simulation

All the material for *Coasters, Etc.* is self-contained in the text-workbook and on the student CD-ROM. As an employee, you need to provide three file folders for organizing your work. Label the folders as follows:

Current Projects (for work in progress)
Completed Projects (for completed tasks)
Stored Documents (for storing source documents as work is completed)

Each of the five projects provides job assignments that can be completed within a week; however, some jobs may be ongoing through additional projects and be completed over a two-to-three-week time frame. The first project contains detailed directions on each new job. As you gain more experience in a particular job, fewer directions are provided. By reading directions and using the reference material you should be able to complete all the assignments.

Since this is an integrated office simulation, you will use a variety of software including word processing, database, spreadsheet, desktop publishing, and presentation graphics. You will also use the computer for electronic communications and research.

Employee Manual

The Employee Manual contains important information about the company, the description and responsibilities of the administrative assistant, and a reference section with guidelines for formatting documents. Read the entire manual before beginning the simulation in order to become familiar with the company and the job responsibilities.

The Employee Manual consists of these sections:

Employee Welcome Letter
Job Description
Job Responsibilities
General Procedures
Reference Materials
    Park Location Map
    Time-Zone Map
    Partial Organization Chart
    Table 1 Sales Representatives

Table 2 Administrative Departments
Wage-Bracket Withholding Tables
Quality Circle Management
Project Evaluation form
Project Worksheet Plan form
Correspondence Guidelines
Sample Letter
Sample Standard Memo
Sample Contemporary Memo
Sample E-mail
Sample Agenda Outline
Sample Minutes of a Meeting
Sample Templates
Letterhead, Memo, Facsimile, E-mail,
To Do list, Notes from Melinda
State and Territory Abbreviations
Proofreader's Marks
Sample Completed Project Worksheet Plan
Sample Completed Project Evaluation
Calendar forms for April, May, June, July, August
(for use if an electronic calendar is not available)

Outline of Projects

Each project includes directions provided through e-mail, Notes from Melinda, To Do lists, and the source documents necessary to complete the tasks. Also included with each project is a Project Worksheet Plan to help you organize the tasks and a Project Evaluation form to help you analyze your work and time management skills. These forms are also provided on the student CD-ROM.

Project 1 March 30–April 3, 20XX
Project 2 April 6–April 10, 20XX
Project 3 April 13–April 17, 20XX
Project 4 April 20–April 24, 20XX
Project 5 April 27–May 1, 20XX

Student CD-ROM

The student CD-ROM includes e-mail messages from Melinda O'Neal, the office manager, that provide you with detailed directions for completing your duties. In addition, e-mail messages from sales representatives or other employees of *Coasters, Etc.* are included for informational purposes. The CD also includes templates, spreadsheets, database, and graphic files that are necessary for the completion of the projects. The template files are provided for the letters, e-mails, facsimiles, project evaluation, and project worksheet plan forms.

Employee Manual

Group Sales Division

★ COASTERS, ETC. ★

March 15, 20XX

Dear New Associate:

Welcome to Coasters, Etc. Amusement Park located near Castle Rock, Colorado, between Denver and Colorado Springs. Coasters, Etc. is owned by Prism Parks International, which also owns three other parks in the United States and one located in Osaka, Japan. Coasters, Etc. provides an exciting work environment for all associates, now numbering over 500, including 400 seasonal park employees. You will find a supportive and a collaborative effort from the entire staff at Coasters.

As part of our commitment to employees, we follow the Prism corporate lead in utilizing Total Quality Management practices. One of our core beliefs is that each person has worthwhile ideas to contribute and should have the opportunity to be heard. We are committed to hiring and training quality personnel in return for quality performance, so our employees receive higher wages, better benefits, and long-term employment. We look forward to a mutually beneficial relationship with you.

As part of the team, you will be excited to know we are planning a grand opening of another new coaster. The latest addition to our coaster arsenal is TurboFlight, a coaster that catapults the riders at 120 miles per hour into four inverted loops, all in the pitch darkness of outer space. We look forward to a successful year of creating excitement in people's lives, by making people happy, and encouraging everyone to have fun. Our goal is to create a memorable experience for our guests and a memorable career for you. We welcome you as one of our new associates.

Sincerely,

Jonathan Wise

Jonathan Wise
Executive Vice President and General Manager

3000 Prism Highway, Castle Rock, CO 80732
1-800-555-3251
Fax: 1-303-555-1212   http://www.prism.coaster.com   E-mail: coasters@prism.com

Job Description

You will be working as an administrative assistant to Melinda O'Neal, Office Manager, in the Group Sales Division, one of six divisions of Marketing. Group Sales is responsible for selling specific "day" outings at the park to companies and organizations. As an administrative assistant, you are responsible for sales support to the Group Sales team. The names and addresses of nine sales representatives are included in Table 1 Sales Representatives in the Reference section of the Employee Manual.

Employees who work in other administrative divisions of Coasters, Etc. and participate in most of the Marketing Division meetings are included in Table 2 Administrative Departments in the Reference section of the Employee Manual.

Job Responsibilities

As an administrative assistant to Melinda O'Neal, you will use a variety of computer software applications including word processing, database, spreadsheet, desktop publishing, and presentation graphics. In addition, electronic communications such as e-mail, facsimile, and the Internet will be used in performing many tasks. You will also need to use good telephone skills to develop positive relationships both internally with other Coasters' employees and externally with customers. The way you handle telephone calls creates an impression of the company and its attitude toward customers. Your attentiveness can help build and maintain good public relations. More specific responsibilities you may assume include:

1. Organize meetings. Prepare agendas, record and distribute minutes, schedule conference room for meetings.
2. Tally daily miscellaneous cash receipts from contracted vendors.
3. Create spreadsheets showing breakdowns and distribution of cash receipts.
4. Prepare promotional material (flyers, posters, forms) and coordinate printing.
5. Prepare databases for major promotions such as Math & Science Day and Grad Nite. (Grad Nite changes to College Night in Project 3.)
6. Compose and edit letters and memorandums.
7. Use spreadsheets to calculate payroll for sales staff.
8. Compute bonus and commission reports for the sales staff.
9. Act as liaison between Group Sales and other Coasters, Etc. departments.
10. Research information on the Internet.
11. Prepare presentations using presentation graphics software.
12. Provide support to the sales staff by sending information to them and their clients as needed.
13. Make reservations for hotel accommodations at local or national sales meetings.

14. Keep a calendar.
15. Maintain good customer relations.

General Procedures

As Administrative Assistant you should follow the basic procedures outlined below. Anything labeled *Administrative Assistant* in your e-mail, In-box, or Notes from Melinda pertains to you. You will find directions for daily tasks to be completed in these documents. Notice that Xs have been used throughout the simulation to indicate the current year. You should replace the Xs with the current year in any documents you key.

Set Up

Prepare three folders for organizing your work. Label the folders as follows: *Current Projects, Completed Projects, Stored Documents*. Key labels for a more professional appearance. Your instructor may provide folders or you may need to provide them.

The calendar will need to be set up. Use the calendars provided to set up information. If you are using the electronic calendar, insert the data from the printed calendars provided. Then enter all items to the calendar as you complete each project. You will be asked to print your calendar from time to time to verify your entries. If you are not using electronic calendaring, use the calendars included in the Employee Manual. Review all information for anything related to the current project.

Daily

1. Check all e-mail messages for the day. Melinda will give you directions for tasks that must be completed. (These directions are located on the student CD-ROM or your e-mail account.)
2. Check your In-box for related material to the e-mail messages, Notes from Melinda, and your own "To Do" list. (These forms are found in the Projects Section of the text/workbook).
3. Check e-mail from all other sources including sales representatives and other departments. You are responsible for sales support to the sales representatives.
4. Refer to the Calendar. Update the calendar as you complete each project. If you have access to an electronic calendar, that would be the preferred method of keeping your schedule. If not, calendar pages are provided for you in the Employee Manual.

Weekly

1. Tally Daily Miscellaneous Cash Receipts envelopes found in your In-box.
2. Prepare a spreadsheet showing sales distributions as indicated on the envelope.

Each project includes e-mail and source documents for tasks to be completed during the week. To start each project follow these steps:

1. Gather information from your e-mail.
2. Refer to In-box materials for that week for source documents.
3. Check additional Notes from Melinda and your To Do List.
4. Use the Project Worksheet Plan to help you organize the work for the week. The Project Worksheet Plan is included in the Projects Section of the text/workbook and on the student CD.
   A. Prioritize work in the order that you think is appropriate.
   B. Organize work for the week.
   C. Place work to be completed in a file folder labeled *Current Projects*.
   D. As the work is completed, place the completed documents in the second folder labeled *Completed Projects*.
   E. Source documents should be stored until the entire simulation is completed. Use the third file folder labeled *Stored Documents*.
5. Prepare the Project Evaluation form found in the Employee Manual and submit to your instructor with the work in the *Completed Projects* folder. This form will help you analyze your work, check for completeness and accuracy, and evaluate your progress. A copy of the Project Evaluation form is also on the student CD. As mentioned in the Welcome letter, Coasters, Etc. follows Quality Management practices. We hold Quality Circle meetings with employees on a regular basis. The Project Evaluation forms may be used at these meetings.

Option: You may save all files on a disk which could be given to the teacher for electronic grading. Create a folder for each project and store completed documents in the assigned folders for each project.

Reference Materials

1. Map 1 Prism Parks International
2. Map 2 Time Zones
3. Chart 1 Partial Organization Chart
4. Table 1 Sales Representatives
5. Table 2 Administrative Departments
6. Wage-Bracket Withholding Tables
7. Quality Circle Management
8. E-mail form
9. Project Evaluation form
10. Project Worksheet Plan form

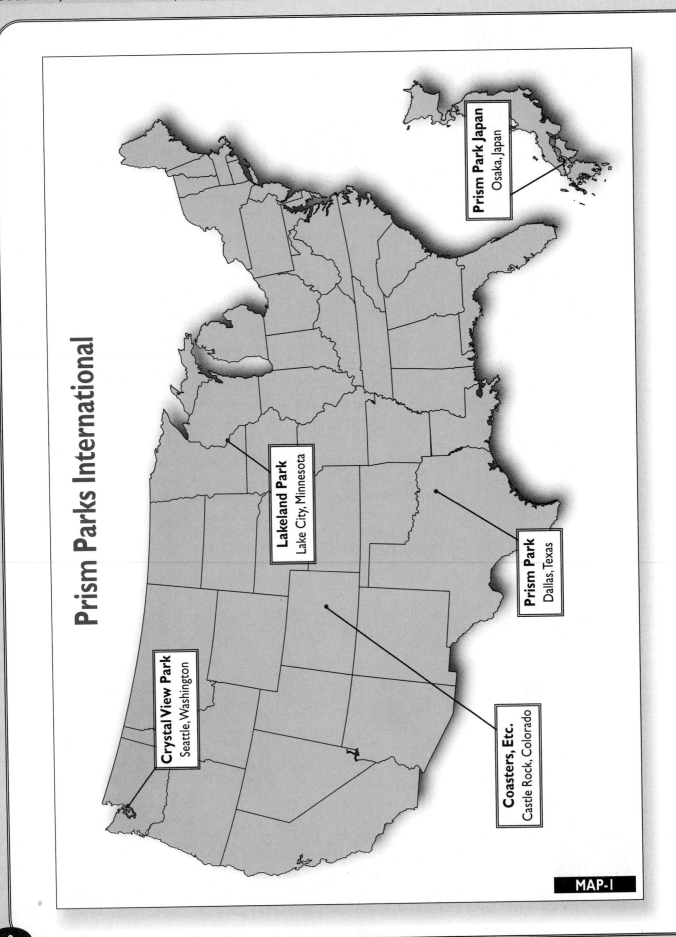

Prism Parks International

Prism Park Japan
Osaka, Japan

Lakeland Park
Lake City, Minnesota

Prism Park
Dallas, Texas

Crystal View Park
Seattle, Washington

Coasters, Etc.
Castle Rock, Colorado

MAP-1

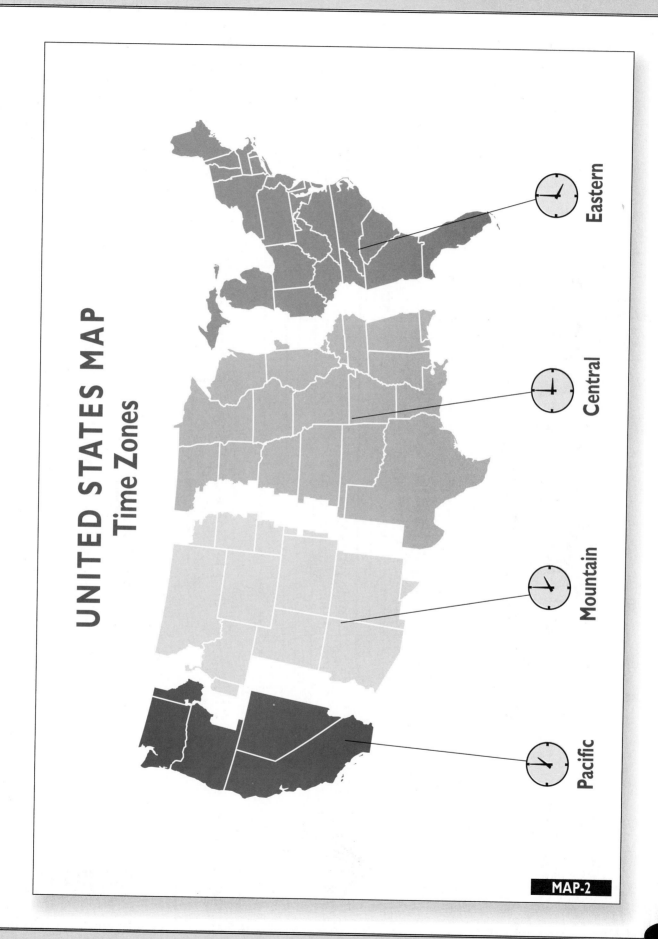

UNITED STATES MAP
Time Zones

Eastern

Central

Mountain

Pacific

MAP-2

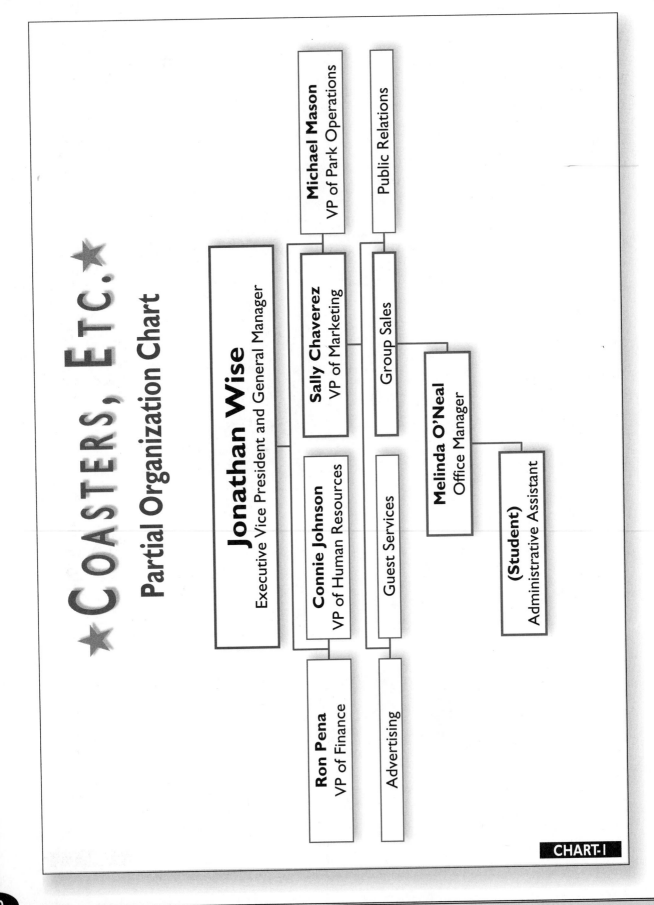

★ COASTERS, ETC.★

Partial Organization Chart

Jonathan Wise
Executive Vice President and General Manager

Michael Mason
VP of Park Operations

Public Relations

Sally Chaverez
VP of Marketing

Group Sales

Connie Johnson
VP of Human Resources

Guest Services

Ron Pena
VP of Finance

Advertising

Melinda O'Neal
Office Manager

(Student)
Administrative Assistant

CHART-1

Table 1—Sales Representatives

Sales Representatives	Territory	Voice Mail/Fax	E-mail
David Alcox 300 Timber Ln. Avon, CO 81620-3251	Northern Colorado	970-555-7693 #22 970-555-7694	alcoxda@prism.com
T.J. Meier 7932 S. Lee St. Loveland, CO 80127-0097	Denver Metropolitan	303-555-1212 #10 303-555-1213	meiertj@prism.com
Ed Alverez 9058 Spruce Grand Junction, CO 81930-0432	Western Colorado	970-555-0193 #32 970-555-0194	alvereej@prism.com
Rich Hoffman 2357 Pikes Peak Ave. Colorado Springs, CO 80907-0392	Colorado Springs Metropolitan	313-555-3242 #51 313-555-3243	hoffmarl@prism.com
Amy Margolies 870 Mt. Adams Ave. Manitou Springs, CO 80150-5253	Eastern Colorado	313-555-2111 #42 313-555-2112	margolai@prism.com
George Schwarz 13 E. Montana Ave. Hayes, KS 67621-9238	Western Kansas	913-555-9993 #101 913-555-9994	schwarge@prism.com
Ron Patterson 800 Maple St. Lincoln, NE 68521-9372	Nebraska/Wyoming	402-555-7900 #102 402-555-7902	patterrn@prism.com
Alvin Lujan 888 Aspen Trails Santa Fe, NM 87501-1234	New Mexico/Texas	505-555-1098 #103 505-555-1099	lujanja@prism.com
David Mattis 900 Lakeside Rd. Salt Lake City, UT 84109-3252	Utah/Arizona	801-555-2303 #104 801-555-2304	mattisdm@prism.com

TABLE-1

Table 2—Administrative Departments

Name	Deparment	Name	Department
Mike Anthony	Math & Science Project	Amy Bird	Business & Industry Rides and Operations
Paul Daniels	Merchandising	Linda Day	Food Service
Jason Jones	Grad Night Project	Steve Kramer	Security
George Luning	Entertainment & Shows	Dan McConnel	Security
Melissa Miller	Rides & Operations	Melinda O'Neal	Group Sales
Jeannie Ryan	Administrative Offices—Administrative Assistant	Carolina Smith	Special Events—Clubs and Organizations
Kevin Wright	Entertainment & Shows	Administrative Assistant	Group Sales

TABLE-2

Wage-Bracket Withholding Tables

MARRIED Persons—MONTHLY Payroll Period

(For Wages Paid Through December 2004)

And the wages are–		And the number of withholding allowances claimed is—										
At least	But less than	0	1	2	3	4	5	6	7	8	9	10
		The amount of income, social security, and Medicare taxes to be withheld is—										
$0	$540	7.65%	7.65%	7.65%	7.65%	7.65%	7.65%	7.65%	7.65%	7.65%	7.65%	7.65%
540	560	$42.08	$42.08	$42.08	$42.08	$42.08	$42.08	$42.08	$42.08	$42.08	$42.08	$42.08
560	580	43.61	43.61	43.61	43.61	43.61	43.61	43.61	43.61	43.61	43.61	43.61
580	600	45.14	45.14	45.14	45.14	45.14	45.14	45.14	45.14	45.14	45.14	45.14
600	640	47.43	47.43	47.43	47.43	47.43	47.43	47.43	47.43	47.43	47.43	47.43
640	680	50.49	50.49	50.49	50.49	50.49	50.49	50.49	50.49	50.49	50.49	50.49
680	720	56.55	53.55	53.55	53.55	53.55	53.55	53.55	53.55	53.55	53.55	53.55
720	760	63.61	56.61	56.61	56.61	56.61	56.61	56.61	56.61	56.61	56.61	56.61
760	800	70.67	59.67	59.67	59.67	59.67	59.67	59.67	59.67	59.67	59.67	59.67
800	840	77.73	62.73	62.73	62.73	62.73	62.73	62.73	62.73	62.73	62.73	62.73
840	880	84.79	65.79	65.79	65.79	65.79	65.79	65.79	65.79	65.79	65.79	65.79
880	920	91.85	68.85	68.85	68.85	68.85	68.85	68.85	68.85	68.85	68.85	68.85
920	960	98.91	73.91	71.91	71.91	71.91	71.91	71.91	71.91	71.91	71.91	71.91
960	1,000	105.97	80.97	74.97	74.97	74.97	74.97	74.97	74.97	74.97	74.97	74.97
1,000	1,040	113.03	88.03	78.03	78.03	78.03	78.03	78.03	78.03	78.03	78.03	78.03
1,040	1,080	120.09	95.09	81.09	81.09	81.09	81.09	81.09	81.09	81.09	81.09	81.09
1,080	1,120	127.15	102.15	84.15	84.15	84.15	84.15	84.15	84.15	84.15	84.15	84.15
1,120	1,160	134.21	109.21	87.21	87.21	87.21	87.21	87.21	87.21	87.21	87.21	87.21
1,160	1,200	141.27	116.27	90.27	90.27	90.27	90.27	90.27	90.27	90.27	90.27	90.27
1,200	1,240	148.33	123.33	97.33	93.33	93.33	93.33	93.33	93.33	93.33	93.33	93.33
1,240	1,280	155.39	130.39	104.39	96.39	96.39	96.39	96.39	96.39	96.39	96.39	96.39
1,280	1,320	162.45	137.45	111.45	99.45	99.45	99.45	99.45	99.45	99.45	99.45	99.45
1,320	1,360	169.51	144.51	118.51	102.51	102.51	102.51	102.51	102.51	102.51	102.51	102.51
1,360	1,400	176.57	151.57	125.57	105.57	105.57	105.57	105.57	105.57	105.57	105.57	105.57
1,400	1,440	183.63	158.63	132.63	108.63	108.63	108.63	108.63	108.63	108.63	108.63	108.63
1,440	1,480	190.69	165.69	139.69	113.69	111.69	111.69	111.69	111.69	111.69	111.69	111.69
1,480	1,520	197.75	172.75	146.75	120.75	114.75	114.75	114.75	114.75	114.75	114.75	114.75
1,520	1,560	204.81	179.81	153.81	127.81	117.81	117.81	117.81	117.81	117.81	117.81	117.81
1,560	1,600	211.87	186.87	160.87	134.87	120.87	120.87	120.87	120.87	120.87	120.87	120.87
1,600	1,640	218.93	193.93	167.93	141.93	123.93	123.93	123.93	123.93	123.93	123.93	123.93
1,640	1,680	225.99	200.99	174.99	148.99	126.99	126.99	126.99	126.99	126.99	126.99	126.99
1,680	1,720	233.05	208.05	182.05	156.05	130.05	130.05	130.05	130.05	130.05	130.05	130.05
1,720	1,760	240.11	215.11	189.11	163.11	137.11	133.11	133.11	133.11	133.11	133.11	133.11
1,760	1,800	247.17	222.17	196.17	170.17	144.17	136.17	136.17	136.17	136.17	136.17	136.17
1,800	1,840	254.23	229.23	203.23	177.23	151.23	139.23	139.23	139.23	139.23	139.23	139.23
1,840	1,880	261.29	236.29	210.29	184.29	158.29	142.29	142.29	142.29	142.29	142.29	142.29
1,880	1,920	270.35	243.35	217.35	191.35	165.35	145.35	145.35	145.35	145.35	145.35	145.35
1,920	1,960	279.41	250.41	224.41	198.41	172.41	148.41	148.41	148.41	148.41	148.41	148.41
1,960	2,000	288.47	257.47	231.47	205.47	179.47	153.47	151.47	151.47	151.47	151.47	151.47
2,000	2,040	297.53	264.53	238.53	212.53	186.53	160.53	154.53	154.53	154.53	154.53	154.53
2,040	2,080	306.59	271.59	245.59	219.59	193.59	167.59	157.59	157.59	157.59	157.59	157.59
2,080	2,120	315.65	278.65	252.65	226.65	200.65	174.65	160.65	160.65	160.65	160.65	160.65
2,120	2,160	324.71	286.71	259.71	233.71	207.71	181.71	163.71	163.71	163.71	163.71	163.71
2,160	2,200	333.77	295.77	266.77	240.77	214.77	188.77	166.77	166.77	166.77	166.77	166.77
2,200	2,240	342.83	304.83	273.83	247.83	221.83	195.83	169.83	169.83	169.83	169.83	169.83
2,240	2,280	351.89	313.89	280.89	254.89	228.89	202.89	176.89	172.89	172.89	172.89	172.89
2,280	2,320	360.95	322.95	287.95	261.95	235.95	209.95	183.95	175.95	175.95	175.95	175.95
2,320	2,360	370.01	332.01	295.01	269.01	243.01	217.01	191.01	179.01	179.01	179.01	179.01
2,360	2,400	379.07	341.07	302.07	276.07	250.07	224.07	198.07	182.07	182.07	182.07	182.07
2,400	2,440	388.13	350.13	311.13	283.13	257.13	231.13	205.13	185.13	185.13	185.13	185.13
2,440	2,480	397.19	359.19	320.19	290.19	264.19	238.19	212.19	188.19	188.19	188.19	188.19
2,480	2,520	406.25	368.25	329.25	297.25	271.25	245.25	219.25	194.25	191.25	191.25	191.25
2,520	2,560	415.31	377.31	338.31	304.31	278.31	252.31	226.31	201.31	194.31	194.31	194.31
2,560	2,600	424.37	386.37	347.37	311.37	285.37	259.37	233.37	208.37	197.37	197.37	197.37
2,600	2,640	433.43	395.43	356.43	318.43	292.43	266.43	240.43	215.43	200.43	200.43	200.43
2,640	2,680	442.49	404.49	365.49	326.49	299.49	273.49	247.49	222.49	203.49	203.49	203.49
2,680	2,720	451.55	413.55	374.55	335.55	306.55	280.55	254.55	229.55	206.55	206.55	206.55
2,720	2,760	460.61	422.61	383.61	344.61	313.61	287.61	261.61	236.61	210.61	209.61	209.61
2,760	2,800	469.67	431.67	392.67	353.67	320.67	294.67	268.67	243.67	217.67	212.67	212.67
2,800	2,840	478.73	440.73	401.73	362.73	327.73	301.73	275.73	250.73	224.73	215.73	215.73
2,840	2,880	487.79	449.79	410.79	371.79	334.79	308.79	282.79	257.79	231.79	218.79	218.79
2,880	2,920	496.85	458.85	419.85	380.85	341.85	315.85	289.85	264.85	238.85	221.85	221.85
2,920	2,960	505.91	467.91	428.91	389.91	350.91	322.91	296.91	271.91	245.91	224.91	224.91
2,960	3,000	514.97	476.97	437.97	398.97	359.97	329.97	303.97	278.97	252.97	227.97	227.97
3,000	3,040	524.03	486.03	447.03	408.03	369.03	337.03	311.03	286.03	260.03	234.03	231.03
3,040	3,080	533.09	495.09	456.09	417.09	378.09	344.09	318.09	293.09	267.09	241.09	234.09
3,080	3,120	542.15	504.15	465.15	426.15	387.15	351.15	325.15	300.15	274.15	248.15	237.15
3,120	3,160	551.21	513.21	474.21	435.21	396.21	358.21	332.21	307.21	281.21	255.21	240.21
3,160	3,200	560.27	522.27	483.27	444.27	405.27	367.27	339.27	314.27	288.27	262.27	243.27
3,200	3,240	569.33	531.33	492.33	453.33	414.33	376.33	346.33	321.33	295.33	269.33	246.33

(Continued on next page)

MARRIED Persons—MONTHLY Payroll Period

(For Wages Paid Through December 2004)

And the wages are–		And the number of withholding allowances claimed is—										
At least	But less than	0	1	2	3	4	5	6	7	8	9	10
		The amount of income, social security, and Medicare taxes to be withheld is—										
$3,240	$3,280	$578.39	$540.39	$501.39	$462.39	$423.39	$385.39	$353.39	$328.39	$302.39	$276.39	$250.39
3,280	3,320	587.45	549.45	510.45	471.45	432.45	394.45	360.45	335.45	309.45	283.45	257.45
3,320	3,360	596.51	558.51	519.51	480.51	441.51	403.51	367.51	342.51	316.51	290.51	264.51
3,360	3,400	605.57	567.57	528.57	489.57	450.57	412.57	374.57	349.57	323.57	297.57	271.57
3,400	3,440	614.63	576.63	537.63	498.63	459.63	421.63	382.63	356.63	330.63	304.63	278.63
3,440	3,480	623.69	585.69	546.69	507.69	468.69	430.69	391.69	363.69	337.69	311.69	285.69
3,480	3,520	632.75	594.75	555.75	516.75	477.75	439.75	400.75	370.75	344.75	318.75	292.75
3,520	3,560	641.81	603.81	564.81	525.81	486.81	448.81	409.81	377.81	351.81	325.81	299.81
3,560	3,600	650.87	612.87	573.87	534.87	495.87	457.87	418.87	384.87	358.87	332.87	306.87
3,600	3,640	659.93	621.93	582.93	543.93	504.93	466.93	427.93	391.93	365.93	339.93	313.93
3,640	3,680	668.99	630.99	591.99	552.99	513.99	475.99	436.99	398.99	372.99	346.99	320.99
3,680	3,720	678.05	640.05	601.05	562.05	523.05	485.05	446.05	407.05	380.05	354.05	328.05
3,720	3,760	687.11	649.11	610.11	571.11	532.11	494.11	455.11	416.11	387.11	361.11	335.11
3,760	3,800	696.17	658.17	619.17	580.17	541.17	503.17	464.17	425.17	394.17	368.17	342.17
3,800	3,840	705.23	667.23	628.23	589.23	550.23	512.23	473.23	434.23	401.23	375.23	349.23
3,840	3,880	714.29	676.29	637.29	598.29	559.29	521.29	482.29	443.29	408.29	382.29	356.29
3,880	3,920	723.35	685.35	646.35	607.35	568.35	530.35	491.35	452.35	415.35	389.35	363.35
3,920	3,960	732.41	694.41	655.41	616.41	577.41	539.41	500.41	461.41	422.41	396.41	370.41
3,960	4,000	741.47	703.47	664.47	625.47	586.47	548.47	509.47	470.47	431.47	403.47	377.47
4,000	4,040	750.53	712.53	673.53	634.53	595.53	557.53	518.53	479.53	440.53	410.53	384.53
4,040	4,080	759.59	721.59	682.59	643.59	604.59	566.59	527.59	488.59	449.59	417.59	391.59
4,080	4,120	768.65	730.65	691.65	652.65	613.65	575.65	536.65	497.65	458.65	424.65	398.65
4,120	4,160	777.71	739.71	700.71	661.71	622.71	584.71	545.71	506.71	467.71	431.71	405.71
4,160	4,200	786.77	748.77	709.77	670.77	631.77	593.77	554.77	515.77	476.77	438.77	412.77
4,200	4,240	795.83	757.83	718.83	679.83	640.83	602.83	563.83	524.83	485.83	447.83	419.83
4,240	4,280	804.89	766.89	727.89	688.89	649.89	611.89	572.89	533.89	494.89	456.89	426.89
4,280	4,320	813.95	775.95	736.95	697.95	658.95	620.95	581.95	542.95	503.95	465.95	433.95
4,320	4,360	823.01	785.01	746.01	707.01	668.01	630.01	591.01	552.01	513.01	475.01	441.01
4,360	4,400	832.07	794.07	755.07	716.07	677.07	639.07	600.07	561.07	522.07	484.07	448.07
4,400	4,440	841.13	803.13	764.13	725.13	686.13	648.13	609.13	570.13	531.13	493.13	455.13
4,440	4,480	850.19	812.19	773.19	734.19	695.19	657.19	618.19	579.19	540.19	502.19	463.19
4,480	4,520	859.25	821.25	782.25	743.25	704.25	666.25	627.25	588.25	549.25	511.25	472.25
4,520	4,560	868.31	830.31	791.31	752.31	713.31	675.31	636.31	597.31	558.31	520.31	481.31
4,560	4,600	877.37	839.37	800.37	761.37	722.37	684.37	645.37	606.37	567.37	529.37	490.37
4,600	4,640	886.43	848.43	809.43	770.43	731.43	693.43	654.43	615.43	576.43	538.43	499.43
4,640	4,680	895.49	857.49	818.49	779.49	740.49	702.49	663.49	624.49	585.49	547.49	508.49
4,680	4,720	904.55	866.55	827.55	788.55	749.55	711.55	672.55	633.55	594.55	556.55	517.55
4,720	4,760	913.61	875.61	836.61	797.61	758.61	720.61	681.61	642.61	603.61	565.61	526.61
4,760	4,800	922.67	884.67	845.67	806.67	767.67	729.67	690.67	651.67	612.67	574.67	535.67
4,800	4,840	931.73	893.73	854.73	815.73	776.73	738.73	699.73	660.73	621.73	583.73	544.73
4,840	4,880	940.79	902.79	863.79	824.79	785.79	747.79	708.79	669.79	630.79	592.79	553.79
4,880	4,920	949.85	911.85	872.85	833.85	794.85	756.85	717.85	678.85	639.85	601.85	562.85
4,920	4,960	958.91	920.91	881.91	842.91	803.91	765.91	726.91	687.91	648.91	610.91	571.91
4,960	5,000	967.97	929.97	890.97	851.97	812.97	774.97	735.97	696.97	657.97	619.97	580.97
5,000	5,040	977.03	939.03	900.03	861.03	822.03	784.03	745.03	706.03	667.03	629.03	590.03
5,040	5,080	986.09	948.09	909.09	870.09	831.09	793.09	754.09	715.09	676.09	638.09	599.09
5,080	5,120	995.15	957.15	918.15	879.15	840.15	802.15	763.15	724.15	685.15	647.15	608.15
5,120	5,160	1,004.21	966.21	927.21	888.21	849.21	811.21	772.21	733.21	694.21	656.21	617.21
5,160	5,200	1,013.27	975.27	936.27	897.27	858.27	820.27	781.27	742.27	703.27	665.27	626.27
5,200	5,240	1,022.33	984.33	945.33	906.33	867.33	829.33	790.33	751.33	712.33	674.33	635.33
5,240	5,280	1,031.39	993.39	954.39	915.39	876.39	838.39	799.39	760.39	721.39	683.39	644.39
5,280	5,320	1,040.45	1,002.45	963.45	924.45	885.45	847.45	808.45	769.45	730.45	692.45	653.45
5,320	5,360	1,049.51	1,011.51	972.51	933.51	894.51	856.51	817.51	778.51	739.51	701.51	662.51
5,360	5,400	1,058.57	1,020.57	981.57	942.57	903.57	865.57	826.57	787.57	748.57	710.57	671.57
5,400	5,440	1,070.63	1,029.63	990.63	951.63	912.63	874.63	835.63	796.63	757.63	719.63	680.63
5,440	5,480	1,083.69	1,038.69	999.69	960.69	921.69	883.69	844.69	805.69	766.69	728.69	689.69
5,480	5,520	1,096.75	1,047.75	1,008.75	969.75	930.75	892.75	853.75	814.75	775.75	737.75	698.75
5,520	5,560	1,109.81	1,056.81	1,017.81	978.81	939.81	901.81	862.81	823.81	784.81	746.81	707.81
5,560	5,600	1,122.87	1,065.87	1,026.87	987.87	948.87	910.87	871.87	832.87	793.87	755.87	716.87
5,600	5,640	1,135.93	1,074.93	1,035.93	996.93	957.93	919.93	880.93	841.93	802.93	764.93	725.93
5,640	5,680	1,148.99	1,083.99	1,044.99	1,005.99	966.99	928.99	889.99	850.99	811.99	773.99	734.99
5,680	5,720	1,162.05	1,097.05	1,054.05	1,015.05	976.05	938.05	899.05	860.05	821.05	783.05	744.05
5,720	5,760	1,175.11	1,110.11	1,063.11	1,024.11	985.11	947.11	908.11	869.11	830.11	792.11	753.11
5,760	5,800	1,188.17	1,123.17	1,072.17	1,033.17	994.17	956.17	917.17	878.17	839.17	801.17	762.17
5,800	5,840	1,201.23	1,136.23	1,081.23	1,042.23	1,003.23	965.23	926.23	887.23	848.23	810.23	771.23

$5,840 and over — Do not use this table. See page 37 for instructions.

Wage-Bracket Withholding Tables

SINGLE Persons—MONTHLY Payroll Period

(For Wages Paid Through December 2004)

And the wages are–		And the number of withholding allowances claimed is—										
At least	But less than	0	1	2	3	4	5	6	7	8	9	10
		The amount of income, social security, and Medicare taxes to be withheld is—										
$0	$220	7.65%	7.65%	7.65%	7.65%	7.65%	7.65%	7.65%	7.65%	7.65%	7.65%	7.65%
220	230	$17.21	$17.21	$17.21	$17.21	$17.21	$17.21	$17.21	$17.21	$17.21	$17.21	$17.21
230	240	18.98	17.98	17.98	17.98	17.98	17.98	17.98	17.98	17.98	17.98	17.98
240	250	20.74	18.74	18.74	18.74	18.74	18.74	18.74	18.74	18.74	18.74	18.74
250	260	22.51	19.51	19.51	19.51	19.51	19.51	19.51	19.51	19.51	19.51	19.51
260	270	24.27	20.27	20.27	20.27	20.27	20.27	20.27	20.27	20.27	20.27	20.27
270	280	26.04	21.04	21.04	21.04	21.04	21.04	21.04	21.04	21.04	21.04	21.04
280	290	27.80	21.80	21.80	21.80	21.80	21.80	21.80	21.80	21.80	21.80	21.80
290	300	29.57	22.57	22.57	22.57	22.57	22.57	22.57	22.57	22.57	22.57	22.57
300	320	32.72	23.72	23.72	23.72	23.72	23.72	23.72	23.72	23.72	23.72	23.72
320	340	36.25	25.25	25.25	25.25	25.25	25.25	25.25	25.25	25.25	25.25	25.25
340	360	39.78	26.78	26.78	26.78	26.78	26.78	26.78	26.78	26.78	26.78	26.78
360	380	43.31	28.31	28.31	28.31	28.31	28.31	28.31	28.31	28.31	28.31	28.31
380	400	46.84	29.84	29.84	29.84	29.84	29.84	29.84	29.84	29.84	29.84	29.84
400	420	50.37	31.37	31.37	31.37	31.37	31.37	31.37	31.37	31.37	31.37	31.37
420	440	53.90	32.90	32.90	32.90	32.90	32.90	32.90	32.90	32.90	32.90	32.90
440	460	57.43	34.43	34.43	34.43	34.43	34.43	34.43	34.43	34.43	34.43	34.43
460	480	60.96	35.96	35.96	35.96	35.96	35.96	35.96	35.96	35.96	35.96	35.96
480	500	64.49	38.49	37.49	37.49	37.49	37.49	37.49	37.49	37.49	37.49	37.49
500	520	68.02	42.02	39.02	39.02	39.02	39.02	39.02	39.02	39.02	39.02	39.02
520	540	71.55	45.55	40.55	40.55	40.55	40.55	40.55	40.55	40.55	40.55	40.55
540	560	75.08	49.08	42.08	42.08	42.08	42.08	42.08	42.08	42.08	42.08	42.08
560	580	78.61	52.61	43.61	43.61	43.61	43.61	43.61	43.61	43.61	43.61	43.61
580	600	82.14	56.14	45.14	45.14	45.14	45.14	45.14	45.14	45.14	45.14	45.14
600	640	87.43	61.43	47.43	47.43	47.43	47.43	47.43	47.43	47.43	47.43	47.43
640	680	94.49	68.49	50.49	50.49	50.49	50.49	50.49	50.49	50.49	50.49	50.49
680	720	101.55	75.55	53.55	53.55	53.55	53.55	53.55	53.55	53.55	53.55	53.55
720	760	108.61	82.61	56.61	56.61	56.61	56.61	56.61	56.61	56.61	56.61	56.61
760	800	115.67	89.67	63.67	59.67	59.67	59.67	59.67	59.67	59.67	59.67	59.67
800	840	123.73	96.73	70.73	62.73	62.73	62.73	62.73	62.73	62.73	62.73	62.73
840	880	132.79	103.79	77.79	65.79	65.79	65.79	65.79	65.79	65.79	65.79	65.79
880	920	141.85	110.85	84.85	68.85	68.85	68.85	68.85	68.85	68.85	68.85	68.85
920	960	150.91	117.91	91.91	71.91	71.91	71.91	71.91	71.91	71.91	71.91	71.91
960	1,000	159.97	124.97	98.97	74.97	74.97	74.97	74.97	74.97	74.97	74.97	74.97
1,000	1,040	169.03	132.03	106.03	80.03	78.03	78.03	78.03	78.03	78.03	78.03	78.03
1,040	1,080	178.09	139.09	113.09	87.09	81.09	81.09	81.09	81.09	81.09	81.09	81.09
1,080	1,120	187.15	148.15	120.15	94.15	84.15	84.15	84.15	84.15	84.15	84.15	84.15
1,120	1,160	196.21	157.21	127.21	101.21	87.21	87.21	87.21	87.21	87.21	87.21	87.21
1,160	1,200	205.27	166.27	134.27	108.27	90.27	90.27	90.27	90.27	90.27	90.27	90.27
1,200	1,240	214.33	175.33	141.33	115.33	93.33	93.33	93.33	93.33	93.33	93.33	93.33
1,240	1,280	223.39	184.39	148.39	122.39	97.39	96.39	96.39	96.39	96.39	96.39	96.39
1,280	1,320	232.45	193.45	155.45	129.45	104.45	99.45	99.45	99.45	99.45	99.45	99.45
1,320	1,360	241.51	202.51	163.51	136.51	111.51	102.51	102.51	102.51	102.51	102.51	102.51
1,360	1,400	250.57	211.57	172.57	143.57	118.57	105.57	105.57	105.57	105.57	105.57	105.57
1,400	1,440	259.63	220.63	181.63	150.63	125.63	108.63	108.63	108.63	108.63	108.63	108.63
1,440	1,480	268.69	229.69	190.69	157.69	132.69	111.69	111.69	111.69	111.69	111.69	111.69
1,480	1,520	277.75	238.75	199.75	164.75	139.75	114.75	114.75	114.75	114.75	114.75	114.75
1,520	1,560	286.81	247.81	208.81	171.81	146.81	120.81	117.81	117.81	117.81	117.81	117.81
1,560	1,600	295.87	256.87	217.87	178.87	153.87	127.87	120.87	120.87	120.87	120.87	120.87
1,600	1,640	304.93	265.93	226.93	187.93	160.93	134.93	123.93	123.93	123.93	123.93	123.93
1,640	1,680	313.99	274.99	235.99	196.99	167.99	141.99	126.99	126.99	126.99	126.99	126.99
1,680	1,720	323.05	284.05	245.05	206.05	175.05	149.05	130.05	130.05	130.05	130.05	130.05
1,720	1,760	332.11	293.11	254.11	215.11	182.11	156.11	133.11	133.11	133.11	133.11	133.11
1,760	1,800	341.17	302.17	263.17	224.17	189.17	163.17	137.17	136.17	136.17	136.17	136.17
1,800	1,840	350.23	311.23	272.23	233.23	196.23	170.23	144.23	139.23	139.23	139.23	139.23
1,840	1,880	359.29	320.29	281.29	242.29	204.29	177.29	151.29	142.29	142.29	142.29	142.29
1,880	1,920	368.35	329.35	290.35	251.35	213.35	184.35	158.35	145.35	145.35	145.35	145.35
1,920	1,960	377.41	338.41	299.41	260.41	222.41	191.41	165.41	148.41	148.41	148.41	148.41
1,960	2,000	386.47	347.47	308.47	269.47	231.47	198.47	172.47	151.47	151.47	151.47	151.47
2,000	2,040	395.53	356.53	317.53	278.53	240.53	205.53	179.53	154.53	154.53	154.53	154.53
2,040	2,080	404.59	365.59	326.59	287.59	249.59	212.59	186.59	160.59	157.59	157.59	157.59
2,080	2,120	413.65	374.65	335.65	296.65	258.65	219.65	193.65	167.65	160.65	160.65	160.65
2,120	2,160	422.71	383.71	344.71	305.71	267.71	228.71	200.71	174.71	163.71	163.71	163.71
2,160	2,200	431.77	392.77	353.77	314.77	276.77	237.77	207.77	181.77	166.77	166.77	166.77
2,200	2,240	440.83	401.83	362.83	323.83	285.83	246.83	214.83	188.83	169.83	169.83	169.83
2,240	2,280	449.89	410.89	371.89	332.89	294.89	255.89	221.89	195.89	172.89	172.89	172.89
2,280	2,320	458.95	419.95	380.95	341.95	303.95	264.95	228.95	202.95	176.95	175.95	175.95
2,320	2,360	468.01	429.01	390.01	351.01	313.01	274.01	236.01	210.01	184.01	179.01	179.01
2,360	2,400	477.07	438.07	399.07	360.07	322.07	283.07	244.07	217.07	191.07	182.07	182.07
2,400	2,440	486.13	447.13	408.13	369.13	331.13	292.13	253.13	224.13	198.13	185.13	185.13

(Continued on next page)

SINGLE Persons—MONTHLY Payroll Period

(For Wages Paid Through December 2004)

And the wages are–		And the number of withholding allowances claimed is—										
At least	But less than	0	1	2	3	4	5	6	7	8	9	10
		The amount of income, social security, and Medicare taxes to be withheld is—										
$2,440	$2,480	$495.19	$456.19	$417.19	$378.19	$340.19	$301.19	$262.19	$231.19	$205.19	$188.19	$188.19
2,480	2,520	504.25	465.25	426.25	387.25	349.25	310.25	271.25	238.25	212.25	191.25	191.25
2,520	2,560	513.31	474.31	435.31	396.31	358.31	319.31	280.31	245.31	219.31	194.31	194.31
2,560	2,600	523.37	483.37	444.37	405.37	367.37	328.37	289.37	252.37	226.37	200.37	197.37
2,600	2,640	536.43	492.43	453.43	414.43	376.43	337.43	298.43	259.43	233.43	207.43	200.43
2,640	2,680	549.49	501.49	462.49	423.49	385.49	346.49	307.49	268.49	240.49	214.49	203.49
2,680	2,720	562.55	510.55	471.55	432.55	394.55	355.55	316.55	277.55	247.55	221.55	206.55
2,720	2,760	575.61	519.61	480.61	441.61	403.61	364.61	325.61	286.61	254.61	228.61	209.61
2,760	2,800	588.67	528.67	489.67	450.67	412.67	373.67	334.67	295.67	261.67	235.67	212.67
2,800	2,840	601.73	537.73	498.73	459.73	421.73	382.73	343.73	304.73	268.73	242.73	217.73
2,840	2,880	614.79	549.79	507.79	468.79	430.79	391.79	352.79	313.79	275.79	249.79	224.79
2,880	2,920	627.85	562.85	516.85	477.85	439.85	400.85	361.85	322.85	284.85	256.85	231.85
2,920	2,960	640.91	575.91	525.91	486.91	448.91	409.91	370.91	331.91	293.91	263.91	238.91
2,960	3,000	653.97	588.97	534.97	495.97	457.97	418.97	379.97	340.97	302.97	270.97	245.97
3,000	3,040	667.03	602.03	544.03	505.03	467.03	428.03	389.03	350.03	312.03	278.03	253.03
3,040	3,080	680.09	615.09	553.09	514.09	476.09	437.09	398.09	359.09	321.09	285.09	260.09
3,080	3,120	693.15	628.15	564.15	523.15	485.15	446.15	407.15	368.15	330.15	292.15	267.15
3,120	3,160	706.21	641.21	577.21	532.21	494.21	455.21	416.21	377.21	339.21	300.21	274.21
3,160	3,200	719.27	654.27	590.27	541.27	503.27	464.27	425.27	386.27	348.27	309.27	281.27
3,200	3,240	732.33	667.33	603.33	550.33	512.33	473.33	434.33	395.33	357.33	318.33	288.33
3,240	3,280	745.39	680.39	616.39	559.39	521.39	482.39	443.39	404.39	366.39	327.39	295.39
3,280	3,320	758.45	693.45	629.45	568.45	530.45	491.45	452.45	413.45	375.45	336.45	302.45
3,320	3,360	771.51	706.51	642.51	577.51	539.51	500.51	461.51	422.51	384.51	345.51	309.51
3,360	3,400	784.57	719.57	655.57	590.57	548.57	509.57	470.57	431.57	393.57	354.57	316.57
3,400	3,440	797.63	732.63	668.63	603.63	557.63	518.63	479.63	440.63	402.63	363.63	324.63
3,440	3,480	810.69	745.69	681.69	616.69	566.69	527.69	488.69	449.69	411.69	372.69	333.69
3,480	3,520	823.75	758.75	694.75	629.75	575.75	536.75	497.75	458.75	420.75	381.75	342.75
3,520	3,560	836.81	771.81	707.81	642.81	584.81	545.81	506.81	467.81	429.81	390.81	351.81
3,560	3,600	849.87	784.87	720.87	655.87	593.87	554.87	515.87	476.87	438.87	399.87	360.87
3,600	3,640	862.93	797.93	733.93	668.93	604.93	563.93	524.93	485.93	447.93	408.93	369.93
3,640	3,680	875.99	810.99	746.99	681.99	617.99	572.99	533.99	494.99	456.99	417.99	378.99
3,680	3,720	889.05	824.05	760.05	695.05	631.05	582.05	543.05	504.05	466.05	427.05	388.05
3,720	3,760	902.11	837.11	773.11	708.11	644.11	591.11	552.11	513.11	475.11	436.11	397.11
3,760	3,800	915.17	850.17	786.17	721.17	657.17	600.17	561.17	522.17	484.17	445.17	406.17
3,800	3,840	928.23	863.23	799.23	734.23	670.23	609.23	570.23	531.23	493.23	454.23	415.23
3,840	3,880	941.29	876.29	812.29	747.29	683.29	618.29	579.29	540.29	502.29	463.29	424.29
3,880	3,920	954.35	889.35	825.35	760.35	696.35	631.35	588.35	549.35	511.35	472.35	433.35
3,920	3,960	967.41	902.41	838.41	773.41	709.41	644.41	597.41	558.41	520.41	481.41	442.41
3,960	4,000	980.47	915.47	851.47	786.47	722.47	657.47	606.47	567.47	529.47	490.47	451.47
4,000	4,040	993.53	928.53	864.53	799.53	735.53	670.53	615.53	576.53	538.53	499.53	460.53
4,040	4,080	1,006.59	941.59	877.59	812.59	748.59	683.59	624.59	585.59	547.59	508.59	469.59
4,080	4,120	1,019.65	954.65	890.65	825.65	761.65	696.65	633.65	594.65	556.65	517.65	478.65
4,120	4,160	1,032.71	967.71	903.71	838.71	774.71	709.71	644.71	603.71	565.71	526.71	487.71
4,160	4,200	1,045.77	980.77	916.77	851.77	787.77	722.77	657.77	612.77	574.77	535.77	496.77
4,200	4,240	1,058.83	993.83	929.83	864.83	800.83	735.83	670.83	621.83	583.83	544.83	505.83
4,240	4,280	1,071.89	1,006.89	942.89	877.89	813.89	748.89	683.89	630.89	592.89	553.89	514.89
4,280	4,320	1,084.95	1,019.95	955.95	890.95	826.95	761.95	696.95	639.95	601.95	562.95	523.95
4,320	4,360	1,098.01	1,033.01	969.01	904.01	840.01	775.01	710.01	649.01	611.01	572.01	533.01
4,360	4,400	1,111.07	1,046.07	982.07	917.07	853.07	788.07	723.07	659.07	620.07	581.07	542.07
4,400	4,440	1,124.13	1,059.13	995.13	930.13	866.13	801.13	736.13	672.13	629.13	590.13	551.13
4,440	4,480	1,137.19	1,072.19	1,008.19	943.19	879.19	814.19	749.19	685.19	638.19	599.19	560.19
4,480	4,520	1,150.25	1,085.25	1,021.25	956.25	892.25	827.25	762.25	698.25	647.25	608.25	569.25
4,520	4,560	1,163.31	1,098.31	1,034.31	969.31	905.31	840.31	775.31	711.31	656.31	617.31	578.31
4,560	4,600	1,176.37	1,111.37	1,047.37	982.37	918.37	853.37	788.37	724.37	665.37	626.37	587.37
4,600	4,640	1,189.43	1,124.43	1,060.43	995.43	931.43	866.43	801.43	737.43	674.43	635.43	596.43
4,640	4,680	1,202.49	1,137.49	1,073.49	1,008.49	944.49	879.49	814.49	750.49	685.49	644.49	605.49
4,680	4,720	1,215.55	1,150.55	1,086.55	1,021.55	957.55	892.55	827.55	763.55	698.55	653.55	614.55
4,720	4,760	1,228.61	1,163.61	1,099.61	1,034.61	970.61	905.61	840.61	776.61	711.61	662.61	623.61
4,760	4,800	1,241.67	1,176.67	1,112.67	1,047.67	983.67	918.67	853.67	789.67	724.67	671.67	632.67
4,800	4,840	1,254.73	1,189.73	1,125.73	1,060.73	996.73	931.73	866.73	802.73	737.73	680.73	641.73
4,840	4,880	1,267.79	1,202.79	1,138.79	1,073.79	1,009.79	944.79	879.79	815.79	750.79	689.79	650.79
4,880	4,920	1,280.85	1,215.85	1,151.85	1,086.85	1,022.85	957.85	892.85	828.85	763.85	699.85	659.85
4,920	4,960	1,293.91	1,228.91	1,164.91	1,099.91	1,035.91	970.91	905.91	841.91	776.91	712.91	668.91
4,960	5,000	1,306.97	1,241.97	1,177.97	1,112.97	1,048.97	983.97	918.97	854.97	789.97	725.97	677.97
5,000	5,040	1,320.03	1,255.03	1,191.03	1,126.03	1,062.03	997.03	932.03	868.03	803.03	739.03	687.03
$5,040 and over		Do not use this table. See page 37 for instructions.										

Quality Circle Management

Coasters, Etc. follows the Quality Management philosophy which includes all employees in the process of Quality Circles.

What is a Quality Circle?

A Quality Circle (QC) is a small group of staff members that meets regularly to solve problems relating to its job scope or workplace. QC works on the basis of a continuous and on-going process in an organization.

The philosophy is that employees will take more interest and pride in their work if they have a share in the decision-making process or have a say in how their work should be conducted. QC gives employees greater satisfaction and motivation.

Benefits of Forming Quality Circles

QCs aim to instill effective team dynamics through communication, trust, shared vision, commitment, involvement, empowerment, and a learning culture among the staff. The benefits are that QCs:

- Promote individual self-development
- Promote teamwork and fellowship
- Improve overall company performance and corporate image

E-Mail

Send To:

From:

Cc: Date:

Subject:

Project Evaluation

Employee Name _____   **Start Date** _____

Project Number _____   **End Date** _____

Write the number of the task and use check marks to indicate that you have completed the following procedures. In the space provided, identify any problems encountered and how you solved them.

Project # & Task # (1-1-1)	Software Used	Spell Checked	Proofread (Grammar & Punctuation)	Accuracy (Dates, Amounts, & Facts)	Neatness (no smudges, tears, or folds)	Formatting Checked (spacing, margins, etc.)	Problem Encountered	Solution

Other Comments

Suggestions or Recommendations _____

Supervisor's Signature _____   **Project Grade** _____

PROJECT WORKSHEET PLAN

Start Date_____   End Date_____

List Items:	Task	Date Needed	Software Required	Estimated Time Needed
___E-mail	_____	_____	_____	_____
	_____	_____	_____	_____
	_____	_____	_____	_____
	_____	_____	_____	_____
	_____	_____	_____	_____
	_____	_____	_____	_____
	_____	_____	_____	_____
	_____	_____	_____	_____
	_____	_____	_____	_____
	_____	_____	_____	_____
___Notes from Melinda	_____	_____	_____	_____
	_____	_____	_____	_____
	_____	_____	_____	_____
	_____	_____	_____	_____
___Other Source Documents	_____	_____	_____	_____
	_____	_____	_____	_____
	_____	_____	_____	_____
___Jobs in Progress	_____	_____	_____	_____
	_____	_____	_____	_____

List the jobs to be completed by priority. Check off as completed.

	Task Completed	Completion Time
___	_____	_____
___	_____	_____
___	_____	_____
___	_____	_____
___	_____	_____
___	_____	_____
___	_____	_____
___	_____	_____

On-going tasks to carry over: _____

_____

Correspondence Guidelines

Format Styles

Coasters, Etc. uses company guidelines for business documents. Follow the company style as you complete your work. A description of the formats is given below. Sample formats and templates are illustrated on the following pages. Several are also on the CD-ROM.

Letter Format

All external business correspondence uses block style with mixed punctuation. The date should be keyed a double-space below the graphic line in the letterhead. Press enter four times after the date before keying the inside address. Use one-inch left and right margins for all letters. Use nine-digit zip codes when available. Leave four blank lines after the complimentary close for the signature block.

The reference initials are typed in lower case followed by a slash and the document identification. For example: mlm/p1-1-1 (project 1 day 1 task 1). Since the order in which the tasks are completed may differ from person to person, use the order of completion as the task reference number. Double space after the reference line for an enclosure notation. Key a copy notation a double space below the enclosure notation or reference line.

Memo Format

Memos are keyed in the standard format using a double space between the header lines TO, FROM, DATE, and SUBJECT. Double space after the SUBJECT line to the body of the memo. Use a two-inch top margin, and one-inch left, right, and bottom margins.

Key the reference line a double space below the last paragraph.

If using a software template or template file from the student CD, key as indicated in the sample memo. A contemporary format that uses double-spaced headings and a graphic is also shown.

E-Mail Format

The e-mail format is established by the software used for sending e-mail and varies in style. Key each paragraph in single spacing blocked at the left margin. Double space between paragraphs. If simulating e-mail, create a template as illustrated in the sample e-mail document.

Envelopes and Address Labels

Use the all-caps style preferred by the United States Postal Service for both envelopes and address labels. Key the return address in the upper left-hand corner two blank lines from the top edge and 0.25 inch from the left edge of the envelope and 0.25 inch from the top. Key the receiver's address 2 inches from the top edge and 4 inches from the left edge of a #10 envelope. Use nine-digit ZIP codes. If one is not available, look up the ZIP code on the U.S.P.O. site on the Internet. If you are using word processing software, the envelope tool may be used to create envelopes.

Agenda and Minutes of a Meeting   The formats for agendas and minutes vary from organization to organization. Sample documents are provided to be used as guidelines.

Facsimile   Facsimiles also vary in format. The template provided on the student CD is the same as the sample facsimile illustrated.

★ COASTERS, ETC. ★

February 21, 20XX   4 returns

Mr. John Smith
Company Title
1000 Busy St.
Anytown, CO 80012   DS 2 returns

Dear Mr. Smith: DS 2 returns

This letter is written in 12-pt Times New Roman. This is the standard typeface and font size for business letters. The letter style is block. This means that all letter parts are keyed at the left margin including the date, inside address, salutation, body, and closing lines. The standard format preferred at Coasters uses mixed punctuation.

Use one-inch left, right, and bottom margins. The top margin should be approximately two inches.

Tables keyed within a letter should be preceded and followed by a double space. The table itself should be singled-spaced. See the example below:

Adult (ages 7–59)	$16.00
Child (ages 3–6, or 48" and under)	$14.00
Seniors (ages 60+)	$14.00
Child (under 3 years)	FREE

See the Employee Manual for formats of other sample documents.   DS 2 returns

Sincerely,   QS 4 returns

Melinda O'Neal, Office Manager
Group Sales Division   DS 2 returns

ref/p1-1-1

3000 Prism Highway, Castle Rock, CO 80732
1-800-555-3251
Fax: 1-303-555-1212   http://www.prism.coaster.com   E-mail: coasters@prism.com

[SAMPLE LETTER]

TO: Jeannie Ryan

FROM: Melinda O'Neal

DATE: June 16, 20XX

SUBJECT: STANDARD MEMO

This memo is keyed in Standard format. The top margin is set at two inches. The heading lines are double-spaced. Each heading is keyed in all caps followed by a colon.

Double space (one blank line) after the subject line. Single space the body of the memo; double space between paragraphs.

Include your reference initials followed by a slash and the project number, day number, and task number.

ref/p1-2-1

[SAMPLE STANDARD MEMO]

Memo  ★COASTERS, ETC.★

TO: Jeannie Ryan

FROM: Melinda O'Neal

DATE: June 16, 20XX

SUBJECT: CONTEMPORARY MEMO FORMAT

This memo may be used as a template and has a contemporary format. You may use this format or create your own. The heading items should be typed in all caps and bold-face followed by a colon and two tabs. Two tabs are used so that the responses for each item align at the left.

Double space between each item in the heading. Begin all paragraphs of the memo at the left margin and key them SS with a DS between paragraphs. Double space after the last paragraph before keying your reference initials and file reference.

ref/p1-2-1

[SAMPLE CONTEMPORARY MEMO]

E-MAIL

To: hoffmarl@prism.com
From: administrative.assistant@coasters.prism.com
Date: April 24, 20XX
Subject: E-Mail Format

E-mail format is similar to an interoffice memo. The heading includes To, From, Date, and Subject (not necessarily in that order). The form varies from software to software.

When keying the address to the sender, key in lowercase, no spaces. It is useful to center or use special indents. You may also do basic inserting and deleting. Most e-mail software has spellcheck. Proofread carefully even if you do have spellcheck.

Always key your name a double space below the text of the last paragraph so it is clear to the receiver who is sending the message.

For the purpose of identifying your e-mail messages in this simulation, use a reference line.

Name
Title
Company

[SAMPLE E-MAIL]

Agenda

Marketing Department
Group Sales Division Meeting

May 3, 20XX
3 p.m.
Conference Room

Announcements

Old Business

Reports

Grad Nite	J. Jones
Math/Science Day	M. Anthony
Special Events Days	C. Smith
Business and Industry	A. Bird

New Business

Suggestions/Concerns/Recommendations
    Account Executives

Adjournment

[SAMPLE AGENDA OUTLINE]

Marketing Department
Group Sales Division Meeting
Minutes
May 15, 20XX

Present:	M. Anthony, A. Bird, P. Daniels, L. Day, R. Hoffman, A. Jenkins, J. Jones, S. Kramer, G. Luning, M. Miller, M. O'Neal, K. Wright, Administrative Assistant
Announcements:	National Sales Meeting is scheduled for August 5, 6, 7 in Orlando, Florida. Details will follow.
	Intra-office electronic mail will go into effect July 1. Training will be held for all employees on June 15. Two sessions will be conducted, one at 8:30 a.m. and another at 1:30 p.m. Sign-up sheets are in the Human Resources office.
Old Business:	None
Reports:	
Grad Nite	J. Jones, Grad Nite coordinator, stated that plans have been finalized. Reservations to date have topped last year's figures by 10 percent and there are still four weeks to go. One question regarding security issues was raised: are more parking lot security personnel needed on Grad Nite? Additional personnel may have to be hired for this event.
Math & Science Day	M. Anthony reported on Math & Science Day figures. Attendance from participating schools is up from last year. He feels the schools are becoming more aware of this educational program and believes next year will be even better. Mr. Anthony suggested that a "Picnic in the Park" be made available and tickets be sold to schools in advance. There are not enough food vendors available on this date since it is a preseason, exclusive event.
Special Events Day	C. Smith stated that the schedule for special events days has been updated and will be available next week. The schedule will be sent to everyone in the Marketing Division as soon as it is printed.

[SAMPLE MINUTES OF A MEETING]

Minutes   -2-   May 15, 20XX

Business and Industry   A. Bird reported that special corporate days were announced
last month. All companies have been notified and will be
announcing the dates to their employees. All companies will
receive discount pricing. There are no "rush orders" for corporate ticketing.

New Business:

Suggestions/Concerns
Recommendations

Account Executives   The sales representatives are eager to know about the laptop
computers. When will they be in? When will the training
begin? Will printing be an issue? These concerns will be
addressed by management, and the representatives will have
their questions answered by voice mail next week.

Adjourned: The meeting was adjourned at 5 p.m. The next meeting will be
June 2, from 3 p.m. to 5 p.m. in the Conference Room.

Respectfully submitted,

A. L. Jenkins

A. L. Jenkins, Administrative Assistant

[SAMPLE MINUTES OF A MEETING]

★Coasters, Etc.★

3000 Prism Highway, Castle Rock, CO 80732
1-800-555-3251
Fax: 1-303-555-1212   http://www.prism.coaster.com   E-mail: coasters@prism.com

[Sample Letterhead Template]

Memo  ★COASTERS, ETC.★

TO:

FROM:

DATE:

SUBJECT:

[SAMPLE MEMO TEMPLATE]

FACSIMILE  **★COASTERS, ETC.★**

TO: [Name of Recipient]

FAX #: [Fax Number]

RE: [Regarding]

DATE: March 30, 20XX

PAGES: [Including cover sheet]

Student's designs may vary if they created their own faxes.

From the desk of . . .

<Name>
<Organization>
<Address>
<City, State, Zip>

<Telephone>
Fax: <Fax>

[SAMPLE FACSIMILE TEMPLATE]

To do...

This Week

–20xx

[SAMPLE TO DO TEMPLATE]

NOTES FROM MELINDA

Occasionally, I will send notes or attach notes to documents.

[SAMPLE NOTE FROM MELINDA]

State and Territory Abbreviations

Alabama	AL	Kentucky	KY	Ohio	OH
Alaska	AK	Louisiana	LA	Oklahoma	OK
Arizona	AZ	Maine	ME	Oregon	OR
Arkansas	AR	Maryland	MD	Pennsylvania	PA
California	CA	Massachusetts	MA	Puerto Rico	PR
Colorado	CO	Michigan	MI	Rhode Island	RI
Connecticut	CT	Minnesota	MN	South Carolina	SC
Delaware	DE	Mississippi	MS	South Dakota	SD
District of Columbia	DC	Missouri	MO	Tennessee	TN
Florida	FL	Montana	MT	Texas	TX
Georgia	GA	Nebraska	NE	Utah	UT
Guam	GU	Nevada	NV	Vermont	VT
Hawaii	HI	New Hampshire	NH	Virgin Islands	VI
Idaho	ID	New Jersey	NJ	Virginia	VA
Illinois	IL	New Mexico	NM	Washington	WA
Indiana	IN	New York	NY	West Virginia	WV
Iowa	IA	North Carolina	NC	Wisconsin	WI
Kansas	KS	North Dakota	ND	Wyoming	WY

Proofreader's Marks

Meaning	Example	Symbol
add space	This decision was supported by all.	#
delete	This decision wass supported by all.	႒
close up	This deci sion was supported by all.	⌒
delete and close up	This deecision was supported by all.	⌒
change	This dacision was supported by all.	/
insert	This decsion was supported by all.	∧
transpose	This decisoin was supported by all.	∩
lowercase	This Decision was supported by all.	/
uppercase	this decision was supported by all.	≡
bold	This decision was supported by all.	〰〰〰
add punctuation	This decision was supported by all.	⊙
stet (let it stand)	This decision was supported by all.	_ _ _ _ _ or stet
move left	This decision was supported by all.	[
move right	This decision was supported by all.	]
center	This decision was supported by all.	] [
align	This decision was supported by all.	//
spell out	This dec. was supported by all.	◯ sp
new paragraph	¶ This decision was supported by all.	¶

PROJECT I WORKSHEET PLAN

Start Date __3-30__   End Date __4-3__

List Items:	Task	Date Needed	Software Required	Estimated Time Needed
✓ E-mail	read manual	3/30-4/1	—	30'
	send memo to sales staff	3/30	Wd Proc	15'
	create events list	3/30	Wd Proc	15'
	create sales staff database	4/2	WB	45'
	mail to each rep.	4/2	—	15'
	reserve conf. room & food service (memo)	3/31	Wd Proc	10'
	(phone, then confirm w/ memo)			
	create agenda	4/3	Wd Proc	10'
	create flyer	4/10	Wd Proc	30'
✓ Notes from Melinda	take minutes Friday	4/3	—	—
	confirm conference room	3/31	memo Wd Proc	10'
	& food service			
	create new teacher letter	4/1		30'
✓ Other Source Documents	Review minutes format	4/3	—	10'
	update calendar	3/30-4/3	calendar	20'
✓ Jobs in Progress	Type minutes, create letter & flyer			

List the jobs to be completed by priority. Check off as completed.

	Task Completed	Completion Time
✓	Read manual	30'
✓	create form	45'
✓	confirmation memos	20'
✓	send memos w. Events list	30'
✓	agenda	15'
✓	create sales database, prepare mailing	65'

On-going tasks to carry over: __minutes & letter & flyer__

Project Evaluation

Employee Name _Molly Smith_

Project Number _1_

Start Date _Feb 1_

End Date _Feb 5_

Write the number of the task and use check marks to indicate that you have completed the following procedures. In the space provided, identify any problems encountered and how you solved them.

Project # & Task # (1-1-1)	Software Used	Spell Checked	Proofread (Grammar & Punctuation)	Accuracy (Dates, Amounts, & Facts)	Neatness (no smudges, tears, or folds)	Formatting Checked (spacing, margins, etc.)	Problem Encountered	Solution
Pj 1-1 forms	Word	✓	✓	✓	✓	✓	none	—
1-1 Memo	"	✓	✓	✓	✓	✓	Composing memo	practice rewrite
1-1 flyer	Word	✓	✓	✓	✓	✓	deciding format	tried dif. layouts & fonts
1-1 memos	Word	✓	✓	✓	✓	✓	none	—
1-3 flyer	Pagemaker	✓	✓	✓	✓	✓	deciding format	looked at sample these & templates closer than I thought!
1-3 forms	Word	✓	✓	✓	✓	✓	none	
1-2 agenda	Word	✓	✓	✓	✓	✓	none	
1-2 form letter	Word	✓	✓	✓	✓	✓	had to review merge procedure	needed more time
1-1 database	NB	✓	✓	✓	✓	✓	none	—

Other Comments

Suggestions or Recommendations _____

Supervisor's Signature _____ **Project Grade** _____

April

Sunday	Monday	Tuesday	Wednesday	Thursday	Friday	Saturday
			1	2	3	4
5	6	7	8	9	10	11
12	13	14	15	16	17	18
19	20	21	22	23	24	25
26	27	28	29	30		

May

Sunday	Monday	Tuesday	Wednesday	Thursday	Friday	Saturday
					1	2
3	4	5	6	7	8	9
10	11	12	13	14	15	16
17	18	19	20	21	22	23
24 / 31	25	26	27	28	29	30

June

Sunday	Monday	Tuesday	Wednesday	Thursday	Friday	Saturday
	1	2	3	4	5	6
7	8	9	10	11	12	13
14	15	16	17	18	19	20
21	22	23	24	25	26	27
28	29	30				

July

Sunday	Monday	Tuesday	Wednesday	Thursday	Friday	Saturday
			1	2	3	4
5	6	7	8	9	10	11
12	13	14	15	16	17	18
19	20	21	22	23	24	25
26	27	28	29	30	31	

August

Sunday	Monday	Tuesday	Wednesday	Thursday	Friday	Saturday
						1
2	3	4	5	6	7	8
9	10	11	12	13	14	15
16	17	18	19	20	21	22
23 / 30	24 / 31	25	26	27	28	29

March 30, 20XX

Project 1—Days One through Five Procedures

March 30, 20XX

In order to complete the tasks in this project, you will need to assemble the following information:

- E-mail messages from Melinda O'Neal, your supervisor, found on the student CD.
- *Notes from Melinda,* written messages from Melinda.
- *In-box* items, source documents needed for completing the tasks.
- *To Do* lists, additional notes to self on tasks.

Detailed directions for completing the tasks are in the e-mail messages and *Notes from Melinda.* The *In-box* items are source documents needed to complete tasks. The *To Do* lists give additional notes to self to complete tasks.

1. Open EM3-30 file from your student CD-ROM. All e-mail messages for the week are dated beginning with 3-30 (March 30) through 4-3 (April 3) and are stored as EM3-30, EM3-31, EM4-1, etc. Most e-mail messages are from Melinda O'Neal, your supervisor. However, print and read all the messages.

2. Next, look at all the In-box forms. *In-box 1-1-1* related to the EM3-30 e-mail message and the Notes from Melinda labeled *Notes 1-1-1* in the student workbook. EM3-30 is an e-mail to you on your first day and relates specifically to any Notes marked *Notes* 1-1-1 (Project 1, Day 1, Task 1) and In-box 1-1-1 (Project 1, Day 1, Task 1).

3. Continue matching e-mail messages with any related Notes and/or In-box documents for the week. EM3-31 provides instructions for various activities for the week. No Notes or In-box items are provided for some days; for example, Day 2. You will need to compare your items for each day to see what you need to do to complete the work.

4. Use the Project 1 Worksheet Plan to organize the tasks for the week. Use the Sample Worksheet Plan in the Reference section as a guide. The forms are also available on the student CD.

5. As each e-mail task and related source documents are reviewed, write on the Worksheet Plan the task to be completed, the date required, software to be used, and the estimated time to complete.

6. When the plan is complete, put the forms in a folder labeled *Current Projects.* Work on one project at a time.

7. Use the bottom part of the Plan to prioritize the jobs. List them in the order you will complete them. Take into consideration when items need to be used, mailed, distributed, etc.

8. Complete each task as directed in the order of priority you choose. Place the completed documents in a folder marked *Completed Projects* and place the source documents and messages in a folder marked *Stored Documents.*

    Option: Save files with a file name that identifies the Project, the day, and the task number. For example, task 3 of Project 1 on day 1 would be saved as p1d1t3. Place all files for Project 1 in a folder named *Project 1.* Repeat this process for all projects. The teacher then has the option of grading documents electronically. Place an electronic copy of the project evaluation in the folder.

9. Any job carried over to the next week (Project 2) should be noted at the bottom of the form in the space provided. Incomplete source documents and tasks should be kept in the *Current Projects* folder.

10. Complete the Project Evaluation form provided for Project 1.

    Repeat this procedure for each day of the week through April 3.

    When all the work for Project 1 is completed, place the Project 1 Worksheet Plan and completed Project Evaluation in the front of the folder marked *Completed Projects* and give the entire folder to your instructor for evaluation.

PROJECT 1

PROJECT 1 WORKSHEET PLAN

Start Date_____   End Date_____

List Items:	Task	Date Needed	Software Required	Estimated Time Needed
___E-mail	_____	_____	_____	_____
	_____	_____	_____	_____
	_____	_____	_____	_____
	_____	_____	_____	_____
	_____	_____	_____	_____
	_____	_____	_____	_____
	_____	_____	_____	_____
	_____	_____	_____	_____
	_____	_____	_____	_____
	_____	_____	_____	_____
___Notes from Melinda				
	_____	_____	_____	_____
	_____	_____	_____	_____
	_____	_____	_____	_____
	_____	_____	_____	_____
___Other Source Documents				
	_____	_____	_____	_____
	_____	_____	_____	_____
	_____	_____	_____	_____
___Jobs in Progress				
	_____	_____	_____	_____
	_____	_____	_____	_____

List the jobs to be completed by priority. Check off as completed.

	Task Completed	Completion Time
____	_____	_____
____	_____	_____
____	_____	_____
____	_____	
____	_____	_____
____	_____	_____
____	_____	_____
____	_____	_____

On-going tasks to carry over: _____

Project Evaluation

Employee Name _____

Project Number _____

Start Date _____

End Date _____

Write the number of the task and use check marks to indicate that you have completed the following procedures. In the space provided, identify any problems encountered and how you solved them.

Project # & Task # (1-1-1)	Software Used	Spell Checked	Proofread (Grammar & Punctuation)	Accuracy (Dates, Amounts, & Facts)	Neatness (no smudges, tears, or folds)	Formatting Checked (spacing, margins, etc.)	Problem Encountered	Solution

Other Comments

Suggestions or Recommendations _____

Supervisor's Signature _____ **Project Grade** _____

PROJECT 1

NOTES FROM MELINDA

– Create a facsimile coversheet template for your use or use the fax file on the student CD. (1-1-1 fax)

– Create a memo template similar to the example in the Reference manual or use the memo file on the student CD. You may use either the standard or contemporary memo. (1-1-1 mem)

– Create a letterhead similar to the sample in the Reference manual or use the ltrhd file on the student CD. (1-1-1 Let)

– Create a database file from the list of the sales representatives in the Employee Manual, Table 1. Use your database software.

  – Include all information given.

  – Print two reports; sort alphabetically by last name. Report 1 should include name, address, city, state, Zip, and territory for each rep. Report 2 should include name, territory, voice mail number, fax number, and e-mail address for each rep.

  – Fax a copy to each of the sales staff.

  – Send me a copy.

  – Keep a copy for your files.

3-30-20xx

Notes 1-1-1

20XX GROUP SALES SPECIAL ~~DAYS/~~EVENTS

For Clubs and Organizations

EVENT	DATES
Band Music Festival	*April* ~~May~~ 20 & 21
Choral Music Festival	April 27 & 28
Girl Scouts	April 27 & 28
Spirit Song - The Newsboys	May 11
Grad Nite - One night only	~~May 17~~ *June 5*
SADD Day	May 15
4-H Day	June 15
~~Science Day (Exclusive)~~	~~May 22~~
& Science Math Day (Exclusive)	May ~~22~~ *20*
Boy Scouts	May 25 & 26 June 22 & 23
~~Baptist Day~~ *Special Olympics Day*	June 1
~~Assemblies of God State Youth~~ *Ecumenical Church Day*	May 18
Dance Days	June 22 & 23
Military Days	June 30, July 1-7
Public Employee Days	June 23-30 July 21-28
Spirit Song - DC Talk	July 6
~~Deaf~~ Awareness Days *Hearing Impaired*	August 10
Cheerleading Competition	August 31, Septmeber 1
Boy Scouts	October 5 & 6
Girl Scouts	October 12 & 13

Try a table format.

Arrange in order by date.

In-box 1-1-1

NOTES FROM MELINDA

The letter to the teachers for Math & Science Day is in your In-box. (1-3-1)

Revise and edit as indicated. You may need to reduce font, margins, spacing to keep the letter to one page.

Both the letters and flyers for Math & Science Day will be mailed on 4-10. Please give me a copy of both by 4-6 for review. I will e-mail you the information to be included on the flyer.

If you have not already done so, confirm the conference room and food service for Friday's meeting. Send me a copy of all memos.

4-1-20xx

Notes 1-3-1

Draft —
rekey & correct as edited.
Use letterhead
Reduce margin & font size
if necessary to fit on 1 page.

April 15, 20XX *(10)*

{Teacher}
{school}
{address}
{city, st zip}

Dear {Teacher}:

You will soon receive information regarding the *Exclusive Math & Science Day* to be held on *[Wednesday,]*
May 3, 20XX. Due to overwhelming success of the program, we request that you
announce the upcoming event to students and give them the enclosed flyers to take home. *[at Coasters, Etc.]* *(20)*

Math & Science Day is a ~~truly~~ unique event at Coaster's Etc. ~~that~~ we are particularly proud
~~of.~~ The joint effort of Educators and Coasters has made this an annual event that ~~truly~~
puts learning into practice. ~~Through the efforts of~~ educational publishers of science and
math books, an activity booklet ~~has been prepared~~ for grade levels K–12 in all areas of
science and math. *[the]* *[of which]* *[have published]* *[appropriate]*

The activities booklet can be purchased ~~at a price of~~ $15 ~~for all activities~~. Since you may
make copies for your students, you will not need to purchase additional materials if you
participate in Math & Science Day in future years. We ~~sincerely~~ want to make this
program as cost-effective as possible for students and teachers. *[for]*

For every 15 students who purchase a $16 ticket, we will include one free admission for *[ital]* *[ital]*
teacher or chaperone. Because not all food vendors will have booths open on this
exclusive day, a special Picnic in the Park is being provided for fast, delicious food at a
great price. For $4.50 each meal will include a hamburger and a hotdog, potato chips,
fruit or ice cream and fruit drink or soft drink. *[or]*

Park admission tickets and food tickets must be purchased in advance. You should receive
your order form and additional information within a week. Don't let this opportunity ~~to~~
slip by ~~this year.~~ Just ask any of the 15,000 people who ~~came~~ last year's Math & Science
Day—you don't want to miss this! *[through our Group Sales office.]* *[attended]* *[year's]*

Sincerely

Melinda O'Neal, Office Manger
Group Sales 3
MO/mlm 1-2-1
Enclosures

P.S. The deadline for placing orders is May 15. Orders placed after May 15 will be held
at "will call" *(12)* *(12)*

NOTES FROM MELINDA

Our next big project is Grad Nite scheduled for Friday, June 5. Make sure it is noted on your calendar. Review the materials for the week; be sure you have items for the week so far.

4-2-20xx

Notes 1-4-1

Import

LOGO

Order Math &
Science Day *Bold*

**Admission
Tickets and
Picnic in the
Park
Tickets**

move down

Today!

12 pt bold

MAY 20, 20XX

20% shade

logo—coaster.wmf—open in document

_____ Yes! I'd like to bring my class to Math & Science Day 20XX at Coasters, Etc. Please send tickets to the address below. Enclosed is a certified check or money order made payable to Coasters, Etc. Math & Science Day. (No cash or personal checks accepted)

School Name _____

Teacher/Coordinator _____

Street Address or P.O. Box _____ City _____

County _____ State _____ Zip _____

Grade Level _____

10 pt

Math & Science Day Admission Tickets *Bold*

FREE Teacher/Chaperone Tickets
(1 Free ticket per 15 tickets ordered)   _____

Students ages 7 and up   _____ x $16.00 = $ _____

Ages 3-6 or 48" and under   _____ x $12.95 = $ _____

Additional Teachers/Chaperones   _____ x $16.00 = $ _____

10 pt

Bold
Number of students attending Math & Science Day using a Season Pass _____

8 pt Bold

Picnic In The Park Tickets
Hamburger or hot dog, potato chips,
ice cream or fruit, and a fruit drink or soft drink _____ x $ 4.50 = $ _____

(All students are encouraged to pre-purchase meal tickets as other food vendors may be closed.)

8 pt

TOTAL PAYMENT ENCLOSED $ _____

Mail this Ticket Order Form along with payment to: Coasters, Etc. Math & Science Day, Group Sales Div., 3000 Prism Highway, Castle Rock, CO 80732

10 pt

For Park Use Only   Date rec'd _____ Check/M.O.# _____ Packets Mailed _____

In-box 1-3-1

MAY 20, 20XX

LOGO → *Import*

Order Math & Science ∧*Way* **Materials**

Today!

Bold 12 pt

10 pt 20% Shade

____Yes! I'd like to bring my class to Math & Science Day 20XX at Coasters, Etc. Please send the materials I've selected to the address below. Enclosed is a certified check or money order made payable to Coasters, Etc. Math & Science Day. (No cash or personal checks accepted) —*8 pt* *10 pt*

School Name _____

Teacher/Coordinator _____

Street Address or P.O. Box _____ City _____

County _____ State _____ Zip _____

Grade Level _____

Before ordering, check the box that applies to you: —*8 pt*

❏ This is my first visit to Math & Science Day. I need the Complete Set of Materials.
❏ I participated in Math & Science Day last year. There is no need to send materials.
❏ I have participated in the past, but need additional materials as listed below.

NOTE: Order one per instructor, then make photocopies of activities for each student

❏ Middle Grades Math Program _____ booklet(s) x $ 5.00 = $ _____
❏ High School Math Program _____ booklet(s) x $ 5.00 = $ _____
❏ Both Math Programs _____ booklet(s) x $10.00 = $ _____

❏ General Science Program: (K-8) _____ booklet(s) x $ 5.00 = $ _____
❏ Physics: Grades 9-12 _____ booklet(s) x $ 5.00 = $ _____
❏ Biology: Grades 9-12 _____ booklet(s) x $ 5.00 = $ _____
❏ All Science Programs _____ booklet(s) x $15.00 = $ _____

10 pt

Mail this Materials Order Form along with payment to: Coasters, Etc. Math & Science Day, Group Sales Div., 3000 Prism Highway, CastleRock, CO 80732 —*8 pt*

20% Shade

For Park Use Only   Date rec'd _____   Check/M.O.# _____   Packets Mailed _____

match ticket order form.

Logo — coaster.wmf

A.A. Please correct as indicated
use Times Roman and point size as marked
Note: this was created in a table.

April 6, 20XX

Project 2—Days One through Five Procedures

April 6, 20XX

In order to complete the tasks in this project, you will need to assemble the following information:

- E-mail messages from Melinda O'Neal, your supervisor, found on the student CD.
- *Notes from Melinda,* written messages from Melinda.
- *In-box* items, source documents needed for completing the tasks.
- *To Do* lists, additional notes to self on tasks.

Detailed directions for completing the tasks are in the e-mail messages and *Notes from Melinda.* The *In-box* items are source documents needed to complete tasks. The *To Do* lists give additional notes to self to complete tasks. If an EM is labeled with an *A* or *B,* such as EM4-6A, and EM4-6B, it means that there are two e-mails on that day, April 6. The first is labeled EM4-6A and the second is labeled EM4-6B.

1. Open EM4-6 file from your student CD-ROM. All e-mail messages for the week are dated beginning with 4-6 (April 6) through 4-9 (April 9) and are stored as EM4-6, EM4-7, EM4-9, etc. Most e-mail messages are from Melinda O'Neal, your supervisor. Print and read all the messages, however.

2. Next, look at all the In-box forms marked *In-box* and the Notes labeled *Notes* in the student workbook. EM4-6A is an e-mail to you and relates specifically to the *In-box 2-1-2* (Project 2, Day 1, Task 2) in the student workbook. You will note that EM4-6A also relates to a project that you worked on in Week 1 (Project 1). Day 2 is EM4-7 and relates specifically to Notes marked *Notes 2-2-1* and *2-2-2; In-box 2-2-1* and *In-box 2-2-2.*

3. Continue matching e-mail messages with any related Notes and/or In-box documents for the week.

4. Use the Project 2 Worksheet Plan to organize the tasks for the week. Use the Sample Worksheet Plan in the Reference section as a guide. The form is also available on the student CD.

5. As each e-mail task and related source documents are reviewed, write on the Worksheet Plan the task to be completed, the date required, software to be used, and the estimated time to complete.

6. When the plan is complete, put the forms in a folder labeled *Current Projects*. Work on one project at a time.

7. Use the bottom part of the Plan to prioritize the jobs. List them in the order you will complete them. Take into consideration when items need to be used, mailed, distributed, etc.

8. Complete each task as directed in the order of priority you choose. Place the completed documents in a folder marked *Completed Projects* and place the source documents and messages in a folder marked *Stored Documents*.

   Option: Save the files with a file name that identifies the project, the day, and the task number. For example, task 3 of Project 2 on day 1 would be saved as p2d1t3. Place all files for Project 2 in a folder named *Project 2*. Repeat this process for all projects. The teacher then has the option of grading documents electronically. Place an electronic copy of the project evaluation in the folder.

9. Any job carried over to the next week (Project 3) should be noted at the bottom of the form in the space provided. Incomplete source documents and tasks should be kept in the *Current Projects* folder.

10. Complete the Project Evaluation form provided for Project 2.

   Repeat this procedure for each day of the week through April 10.

   When all the work for Project 2 is completed, place the Project 2 Worksheet Plan and completed Project Evaluation in the front of the folder marked *Completed Projects* and give the entire folder to your instructor for evaluation.

PROJECT 2 WORKSHEET PLAN

Start Date_____   End Date_____

List Items:	Task	Date Needed	Software Required	Estimated Time Needed
___E-mail	_____	_____	_____	_____
	_____	_____	_____	_____
	_____	_____	_____	_____
	_____	_____	_____	_____
	_____	_____	_____	_____
	_____	_____	_____	_____
	_____	_____	_____	_____
	_____	_____	_____	_____
	_____	_____	_____	_____
	_____	_____	_____	_____
___Notes from Melinda				
	_____	_____	_____	_____
	_____	_____	_____	_____
	_____	_____	_____	_____
	_____	_____	_____	_____
___Other Source Documents				
	_____	_____	_____	_____
	_____	_____	_____	_____
	_____	_____	_____	_____
___Jobs in Progress				
	_____	_____	_____	_____
	_____	_____	_____	_____

List the jobs to be completed by priority. Check off as completed.

	Task Completed	Completion Time
____	_____	_____
____	_____	_____
____	_____	_____
____	_____	_____
____	_____	_____
____	_____	_____
____	_____	_____
____	_____	_____
____	_____	_____

On-going tasks to carry over: _____

_____

Project Evaluation

Employee Name _____   **Start Date** _____

Project Number _____   **End Date** _____

Write the number of the task and use check marks to indicate that you have completed the following procedures. In the space provided, identify any problems encountered and how you solved them.

Project # & Task # (1-1-1)	Software Used	Spell Checked	Proofread (Grammar & Punctuation)	Accuracy (Dates, Amounts, & Facts)	Neatness (no smudges, tears, or folds)	Formatting Checked (spacing, margins, etc.)	Problem Encountered	Solution

Other Comments

Suggestions or Recommendations _____

Supervisor's Signature _____   **Project Grade** _____

Minutes

Attendance: M. Anthony, A. Bird, P. Daniels, L. Day, J. Jones, S. Kramer, G. Luning, D. McConnel, M. Miller, M. O'Neal, C. Smith, K. Wright.

Announcements: Review of previous season special events figures and projections for the coming year.

Old Business: None

Reports:

italics & cap   *italics & cap*

Grad Nite— J. Jones discussed the possibility of changing grad nite in June to college night. Of all the special events groups listed, this is one target area that is completely missing from any special event. High schools and elementary schools have a number of special days. Business and industry are also prevalent on the Events calendar. College-age students are not only one of our highest employees categories, but are also a highly supportive amusement park group. The number of colleges, not only in the immediate area, but also in surrounding states, warrants some special events day. This change was supported by a unanimous vote of the six Marketing divisions and will be suggested to Management for immediate consideration this year. Promotion will begin in the next few weeks if management agrees.

Math & Science Day— M. Anthony reported on the overall progress for Math & Science Day to be held May 20. He stated that reservations are coming in at a faster rate than last year.

Other members of this committee reported as follows:

P. Daniels Merchandising. Front gates will open at 9:00 *8:30* a.m. International Street shops will open at 9 a.m.

S. Kramer Security. A clearance list for groups will be given to admissions. Additional parking lot security will be added because of the number of buses expected. Front Gate Policy. *lc & new paragraph* Math and Science Day is an exclusive event; therefore, the park is closed to the general public. Every one entering the park must possess a Science and Math Day admission *present*

In-box 2-1-2

ticket. Season Pass holders must have the special Math & Science Day ticket along with their actual Season Pass card. Other Season Pass holders may not be admitted.

D. McConnel   Security. Please let me know if there are any unusual first-aid needs or student-related disability problems.

M. O'Neal   Group Sales. Please schedule two associates to work the Will Call Windows from 8:15 to 11:00 a.m. We will call Linda Day with the final food guarantee on Friday, May 15, and update daily if necessary.

G. Luning   Entertainment & Shows. Please have characters available in the morning at the Front Gate from 9:00 a.m. till 11:00 a.m. Please see the special event form for picnic grove requests. Also, please make sure TV is up and running.

The DeeJay is scheduled for 5:30 p.m. to 7:30 p.m. at the International (St.) Pavilion and at the waiting area for the Devil's Backbone coaster ride, from 1:30 p.m.–3:00 p.m.

Special Events days—   C. Smith confirmed the tentative list of special events for clubs and organizations. She expects to be adding about five more to the list as soon as the request forms from those clubs and organizations are returned. This year's deadline for the request is May 1 in order to be added to the calendar.

Business & Industry—   A. Bird who is in the process of completing the Business & Industry special events list for her clients. The sales representatives are working on this with Amy. She expects this list to be completed by June 1.

New Business:

Suggestions/Concerns/Contributions

Account Executives—seem to be having no trouble getting used to the laptop computers. They are especially happy about how much easier it is to compare reports on time.
complete

Adjournment   The meeting was adjourned at 5:00 p.m.

Submitted by: (administrative assistant)

In-box 2-1-2

A.A. – Set up the spreadsheet something like this. Format with color and shading.

Headings centered:

Miscellaneous Cash Receipts

For Week Ending April 5, 20xx

Account to Credit	Currency	Corn	Checks	Visa/MC	Gift Cert.	Bucks	Totals
Key Photos	589.—	125.—	790.—	—	150.—	50.—	
Cotton Candy	218.—	282.—	—	—	—	15.—	
Lemon Ice	375.—	100.—	—	—	—	—	
Ice Cream	75.—	50.—	—	—	—	25.—	
Belgian Waffles	420.—	179.—	115.—	—	70.—	15.—	
Balloons	170.—	150.—	45.—	—	25.—	19.—	
NiteGlo Rings	200.—	89.—	17.—	—	36.—	10.—	
Totals							

1. Complete the spreadsheet.
2. Verify envelope totals against distribution summary sheet.
3. Create a pie chart showing distribution and percentage of each account.

In-box 2-2-1

★COASTERS, ETC.★

Miscellaneous Cash Receipts

Miscellaneous Cash Receipts Envelope

SIGNATURES

DEPARTMENT: _____
RECEIVED BY: _____

Date _4-5-20xx_

ACCOUNT TO CREDIT	DESCRIPTION	AMOUNT
Key Photos	Promotional Sales 500	1704.00
Cotton Candy	Food Sales 600	515.00
Lemon Ice	Food Sales 610	475.00
Ice Cream	Food Sales 620	150.00
Bel. Waffles	Food Sales 650	799.00
Balloons	Promotional Sales 530	409.00
NiteGlo Rings	Promotional Sales 570	352.00
	Total	

UNIT	CURRENCY
$100	900.00
50	500.00
20	300.00
10	250.00
5	75.00
2	4.00
1	18.00
TOTAL	2047.00

UNIT	COIN
$1.00	75.00
.50	60.00
.25	462.00
.10	250.00
.05	116.00
.01	12.00
ROLL COIN	———
TOTAL	975.00

TOTAL CURRENCY	$_____
TOTAL.COIN	$_____
TOTAL CHECKS	$967.00
VISA/MC	$———
GIFT CERTIFICATES	$281.00
SCREAMIN' BUCKS	$134.00
_____	$_____
_____	$_____
TOTAL	$_____

For auditor's use only:

Auditor:

Debits: $_____   Credits: $_____   Over (short): $_____

In-box 2-2-1

Distribution Summary

Cash Receipts—Key Photos		
April 5, 20XX		
Currency		$589.00
Coins		125.00
Checks		790.00
VISA/MC		0.00
Gift Certificates		150.00
Bucks		50.00
Total Receipts		$1,704.00

Cash Receipts—Cotton Candy		
April 5, 20XX		
Currency		$218.00
Coins		282.00
Checks		0.00
VISA/MC		0.00
Gift Certificates		0.00
Bucks		15.00
Total Receipts		$515.00

Cash Receipts—Lemon Ice		
April 5, 20XX		
Currency		$375.00
Coins		100.00
Checks		0.00
VISA/MC		0.00
Gift Certificates		0.00
Bucks		0.00
Total Receipts		$475.00

Cash Receipts—Ice Cream		
April 5, 20XX		
Currency		$75.00
Coins		50.00
Checks		0.00
VISA/MC		0.00
Gift Certificates		0.00
Bucks		25.00
Total Receipts		$150.00

Cash Receipts—Belgian Waffles		
April 5, 20XX		
Currency		$420.00
Coins		179.00
Checks		115.00
VISA/MC		0.00
Gift Certificates		70.00
Bucks		15.00
Total Receipts		$799.00

Cash Receipts—Balloons		
April 5, 20XX		
Currency		$170.00
Coins		150.00
Checks		45.00
VISA/MC		0.00
Gift Certificates		25.00
Bucks		19.00
Total Receipts		$409.00

Cash Receipts—NiteGlo Rings		
April 5, 20XX		
Currency		$200.00
Coins		89.00
Checks		17.00
VISA/MC		0.00
Gift Certificates		36.00
Bucks		10.00
Total Receipts		$352.00

Cash Receipts—TurboFlight Tee		
April 5, 20XX		
Currency		
Coins		
Checks		
VISA/MC		
Gift Certificates		
Bucks		
Total Receipts		

Cash Receipts—TurboFlight Key		
April 5, 20XX		
Currency		
Coins		
Checks		
VISA/MC		
Gift Certificates		
Bucks		
Total Receipts		

Totals		
Currency		$2,047.00
Coins		975.00
Checks		967.00
VISA/MC		0.00
Gift Certificates		281.00
Bucks		134.00
		$4,404.00
Totals		$4,404.00

In-box 2-2-1

Notes from Melinda

Marketing would like to see Quarters 1-4 of last year's figures for Group Sales.

Please make a spreadsheet from the table in your In-box. Complete calculations on the spreadsheet.

Create a bar chart so they can compare quarters.

Thanks,
Melinda

(Alphabetize by representative's last name)

4-7-20xx

Notes 2-2-1

GROUP SALES FIGURES
(previous year)

Sales Representative	Qtr. 1	Qtr. 2	Qtr. 3	Qtr. 4	Total
Alcox, David	75,250	120,800	115,300	50,750	
Meier, T.J.	50,670	80,190	75,900	67,000	
Alverez, Ed	112,350	140,550	125,000	95,000	
Hoffman, Rich	72,000	95,500	106,300	87,300	
Margolies, Amy	67,890	110,250	94,500	85,650	
Schwarz, George	30,140	63,075	71,200	65,720	
Patterson, Ron	57,800	94,300	87,500	85,800	
Lujan, Alvin	93,600	125,200	126,300	72,000	
Mattis, David	85,400	130,300	115,000	91,100	
Totals					

A.A.– Create a spreadsheet in this format. Include column totals and totals by rep. Use currency format. The "totals" should display a dollar sign ($). Create a bar chart to compare quarters.

In-box 2-2-2

NOTES FROM MELINDA

Marketing needs another report on group sales. They need a spreadsheet showing each quarter with breakdown by category.

See your In-box for table by category and create charts as directed.

Thanks again
Melinda

P.S. Calculated totals should agree with sales figures by representative total.

4-7-20xx

Notes 2-2-2

Group Sales by Category
(~~current~~ year)
previous

Sales Category	Qtr. 1	Qtr. 2	Qtr. 3	Qtr. 4	Total
Schools/Colleges	250,100.51	277,142.31	400,517.15	457,952.05	
Clubs/Organizations	92,300.28	138,019.59	303,968.20	45,777.23	
Business/Industry	260,698.78	494,871.43	183,921.53	188,412.38	
Exclusives	42,000.43	50,131.67	28,593.12	8,178.34	
Totals					

Create a spreadsheet based on figures above, format correctly. Create a bar chart showing quarterly breakdown and a pie chart showing breakdown by category. Round to whole numbers and insert commas appropriately for currency.

In-box 2-2-2

Add these colleges to the College Database

Grand Canyon University
3300 W. Camelback Rd.
Phoenix, AZ 85017
602-589-2855
http://www.grand.canyon.edu

Enrollment: 1,242

University of Nebraska–Omaha
60th and Dodge Streets
Omaha, NE 68182
402-554-2800
http://www.unomaha.edu

Enrollment: 7,879

University of Colorado–Colorado Springs
P.O. Box 7150
Austin Bluffs Pkwy.
Colorado Springs, CO 80933
719-593-3383
http://www.uccs.edu

Enrollment: 5,885

Fort Lewis College
100 Rim Drive
Durango, CO 81301
970-247-7010
http://www.fortlewis.edu

Enrollment: 4,217

Emporia State University
1200 Commercial Hwy.
Emporia, KS 66801
316-341-1200
http://www.emporia.edu

Enrollment: 5,600

University of Kansas
126 Strong Blvd.
Lawrence, KS 66045
913-864-3911
http://www.ukans.edu

Enrollment: 19,845

University of Nevada–Las Vegas
4505 Maryland Pkwy.
Las Vegas, NV 89154
702-895-3011
http://www.unlv.edu

Enrollment: 27,000

In-box 2-4-1

NOTES FROM MELINDA

While you're searching the Internet for roller coaster information, see what information you can find on the upcoming Amusement Park Safety Seminar. Amusement Industry Manufacturers & Suppliers (AIMS) usually lists details of this seminar.

I'll need the date, location, hotel, travel information, and seminar information.

Let me know by e-mail what you find out.

Melinda

4-9-20xx

Notes 2-4-1

April 13, 20XX

PROJECT 3

Project 3—Days One through Five Procedures

April 13, 20XX

In order to complete the tasks in this project, you will need to assemble the following information:

- E-mail messages from Melinda O'Neal, your supervisor, found on the student CD.
- *Notes from Melinda,* written messages from Melinda.
- *In-box* items, source documents needed for completing the tasks.
- *To Do* lists, additional notes to self on tasks.

Detailed directions for completing the tasks are in the e-mail messages and *Notes from Melinda.* The *In-box* items are source documents needed to complete tasks. The *To Do* lists give additional notes to self to complete tasks.

1. Open EM4-13 file from your student CD-ROM. All e-mail messages for the week are dated beginning with 4-13 (April 13) through 4-15 (April 15) and are stored as EM4-13, EM4-14, EM 4-15, etc. Most e-mail messages are from Melinda O'Neal, your supervisor. Print and read all the messages, however.

2. Next, look at all the In-box forms marked *In-box 3-1-1* that are related to the EM4-13 e-mail message and the *Notes from Melinda* labeled *Notes 3-1-1* in the student workbook. EM4-13 is an e-mail to you and relates specifically to the *Notes* marked *Notes 3-1-1* (Project 3, Day 1, Task 1) and/or *In-box 3-1-1* (Project 3, Day 1, Task 1). Day 2 is EM4-14 and relates specifically to *Notes* marked *Notes* 3-2-1 and 3-2-2.

3. Continue matching e-mail messages with any related Notes and/or In-box documents for the week.

4. Use the Project 3 Worksheet Plan to organize the tasks for the week. Use the Sample Worksheet Plan in the Reference section as a guide. The form is also available on the student CD.

5. As each e-mail task and related source documents are reviewed, write on the Worksheet Plan the task to be completed, the date required, software to be used, and the estimated time to complete.

6. When the plan is complete, put the forms in a folder labeled *Current Projects.* Work on one project at a time.

7. Use the bottom part of the Plan to prioritize the jobs. List them in the order you will complete them. Take into consideration when items need to be used, mailed, distributed, etc.

8. Complete each task as directed in the order of priority you choose. Place the completed documents in a folder marked *Completed Projects* and place the source documents and messages in a folder marked *Stored Documents*.

   Option: Save the files with a file name that identifies the Project, the day, and the task number. For example, task 3 of Project 3 on day 1 would be saved as p3d1t3. Place all files for Project 3 in a folder named *Project 3*. Repeat this process for all projects. The teacher then has the option of grading documents electronically. Place an electronic copy of the project evaluation in the folder.

9. Any job carried over to the next week (Project 4) should be written at the bottom of the form in the space provided. Incomplete source documents and tasks should be kept in the *Current Projects* folder.

10. Complete the Project Evaluation form provided for Project 3. This form is also available on the student CD.

Repeat this procedure for each day of the week through April 17.

When all the work for Project 3 is completed, place the Project 3 Worksheet Plan and completed Project Evaluation in the front of the folder marked *Completed Projects* and give the entire folder to your instructor for evaluation.

PROJECT 3 WORKSHEET PLAN

Start Date_____   End Date_____

List Items:	Task	Date Needed	Software Required	Estimated Time Needed
___E-mail	_____	_____	_____	_____
	_____	_____	_____	_____
	_____	_____	_____	_____
	_____	_____	_____	_____
	_____	_____	_____	_____
	_____	_____	_____	_____
	_____	_____	_____	_____
	_____	_____	_____	_____
	_____	_____	_____	_____
	_____	_____	_____	_____
___Notes from Melinda	_____	_____	_____	_____
	_____	_____	_____	_____
	_____	_____	_____	_____
___Other Source Documents	_____	_____	_____	_____
	_____	_____	_____	_____
	_____	_____	_____	_____
___Jobs in Progress	_____	_____	_____	_____
	_____	_____	_____	_____

List the jobs to be completed by priority. Check off as completed.

	Task Completed	Completion Time
____	_____	_____
____	_____	_____
____	_____	_____
____	_____	_____
____	_____	_____
____	_____	_____
____	_____	_____

On-going tasks to carry over: _____

_____

Project Evaluation

Employee Name _____ Start Date _____

Project Number _____ End Date _____

Write the number of the task and use check marks to indicate that you have completed the following procedures. In the space provided, identify any problems encountered and how you solved them.

Project # & Task # (1-1-1)	Software Used	Spell Checked	Proofread (Grammar & Punctuation)	Accuracy (Dates, Amounts, & Facts)	Neatness (no smudges, tears, or folds)	Formatting Checked (spacing, margins, etc.)	Problem Encountered	Solution

Other Comments

Suggestions or Recommendations _____

Supervisor's Signature _____ Project Grade _____

NOTES FROM MELINDA

Here are some additional instructions for completing the payroll register.

1. The sales commission figures are in your In-box. Enter new figures, bonuses, and calculate commissions earned on the partial spreadsheet file (comshell). Save as commarch (for March commissions).

2. Transfer figures from the March Commission for Commission and Bonus Earned to the Payroll Register (payshell).

3. Calculate total salary and commission.

4. Calculate New Year-to-Date Earnings.

5. Use the Federal Income Tax Table in the Employee Manual to determine the Federal Income tax.

6. Calculate the Social Security and Medicare taxes.
   - Social Security tax of 6.2% is based on the total earnings up to $87,900 with a maximum tax of $5,394.
   - Medicare is 1.45% of total earnings without limit for every pay period.

7. Calculate the Total Deductions.

8. Calculate the Net Pay.

9. Format the spreadsheet and complete the payroll register.

10. Save as paymarch (for March payroll).

11. Send me a copy for review.

12. Make copies for Marketing, Payroll, and Group Sales.

4-13-20xx

Notes 3-1-1

Sales Commissions
For March Sales

Name	Number of Allowances	Marital Status	Resident State	Year-to-Date Sales	Group Sales	Commission Rate	Commission Earned	Year-to-Date Sales	Bonus Earned	Com. + Bonus Earned
Alcox, David	6	M	CO	98,700	14,300					
Alverez, Ed	5	M	CO	57,000	11,700					
Hoffman, Rich	2	M	CO	87,500	14,300					
Lujan, Alvin	7	M	NM	75,900	13,500					
Margolies, Amy	1	S	CO	102,500	8,700					
Mattis, David	4	M	UT	95,900	5,800					
Meier, T. J.	2	M	CO	69,000	8,500					
Patterson, Ron	1	S	NE	91,800	11,200					
Schwarz, George	3	M	KS	63,100	5,400					
TOTALS										

Commission Schedule:

Group Sales Between		
$ 5,000–$ 6,999	5%	
$ 7,000–$ 9,999	7%	
$10,000–$14,999	8%	
$15,000–$19,999	10%	

When Year-to-Date reaches	$100,000 add $ 1,000 bonus
	$150,000 add $ 5,000 bonus
	$200,000 add $10,000 bonus

In-box 3-1-1

Payroll Register
April 17, 20XX

| Name | Allow-ances | Marital Status | Resident State | EARNINGS | | | | | DEDUCTIONS | | | | | | | |
				Salary	Com. & Bonus	Total	Year-to-Date Earnings	New Y/D Earnings	Fed. Inc. Tax	Soc. Sec. Tax	Medi. Tax	Health Ins.	United Way	Savings	Total Ded.	Net Pay
Alcox, David	6	M	CO	3460			18,500					25.00	5.00			
Alverez, Ed	5	M	CO	3000			12,380									
Hoffman, Rich	2	M	CO	3460			19,690					13.00	5.00			
Lujan, Alvin	7	M	NM	3460			15,600							25.00		
Margolies, Amy	1	S	CO	3330			15,300									
Mattis, David	4	M	UT	3460			14,400					13.00				
Meier, T. J.	2	M	CO	3330			16,500						10.00	20.00		
Patterson, Ron	1	S	NE	3000			14,700						10.00			
Schwarz, George	3	M	KS	3000			11,030					25.00	5.00			
TOTALS																

Add figures from March commission report-spreadsheet.

See Fed. Income Tax Table in Employee Manual Reference

6.2% ↖

1.45%

Note: Social Security tax of 6.2% is based on total earnings up to $87,900—check current amount in Tax guide.

Medicare is 1.45% of total earnings for every pay period.

E-mail copy to Marketing Payroll Group Sales

In-box 3-1-1

★COASTERS, ETC.★

Miscellaneous Cash Receipts Envelope

SIGNATURES

DEPARTMENT: _____
RECEIVED BY: _____

Miscellaneous Cash Receipts

Date 4-12-20xx

ACCOUNT TO CREDIT	DESCRIPTION	AMOUNT
Key Photos	Promotional Sales 500	2430.22
Balloons	Promotional Sales 530	520.91
NiteGlo Rings	Promotional Sales 570	425.54
Ice Cream	Food Sales 620	315.60
Lemon Ice	Food Sales 610	525.21
TurboFlight Tee	Promotional Sales 510	4650.60
TurboFlight Key	Promotional Sales 515	1725.75
Belgian Waffles	Food Sales 650	1300.83
	Total	11,894.70

UNIT	CURRENCY	UNIT	COIN		
$100	400.00	$1.00	1360.00	TOTAL CURRENCY $	4229.00
50	1000.00	.50	683.50	TOTAL COIN $	2975.78
20	1220.00	.25	475.00	TOTAL CHECKS $	2835.10
10	980.00	.10	264.00	VISA/MC $	2614.82
5	540.00	.05	175.65	GIFT CERTIFICATES $	235.00
2	6.00	.01	17.63	SCREAMIN' BUCKS $	5.00
1	83.00	ROLL COIN —		_____ $ _____	
TOTAL	4229.00	TOTAL	2975.78	_____ $ _____	
				TOTAL $	12,894.70

For auditor's use only: Auditor:

Debits: $12894.70   Credits: $11894.70   Over (short): $ (1000)

A.A.—verify and correct please check

In-box 3-1-4

Distribution Summary

Cash Receipts—Key Photos		
April 12, 20XX		
Currency		$771.00
Coins		354.30
Checks		450.00
VISA/MC		829.92
Gift Certificates		25.00
Bucks		0.00
Total Receipts		$2,430.22

Cash Receipts—Cotton Candy		
April 12, 20XX		
Currency		
Coins		
Checks		
VISA/MC		
Gift Certificates		
Bucks		
Total Receipts		

Cash Receipts—Lemon Ice		
April 12, 20XX		
Currency		$290.00
Coins		55.91
Checks		0.00
VISA/MC		164.30
Gift Certificates		10.00
Bucks		5.00
Total Receipts		$525.21

Cash Receipts—Ice Cream		
April 12, 20XX		
Currency		$175.00
Coins		84.55
Checks		31.00
VISA/MC		25.05
Gift Certificates		0.00
Bucks		0.00
Total Receipts		$315.60

Cash Receipts—Belgian Waffles		
April 12, 20XX		
Currency		$218.00
Coins		50.83
Checks		300.00
VISA/MC		712.00
Gift Certificates		20.00
Bucks		0.00
Total Receipts		$1,300.83

Cash Receipts—Balloons		
April 12, 20XX		
Currency		$180.00
Coins		190.18
Checks		95.13
VISA/MC		50.60
Gift Certificates		5.00
Bucks		0.00
Total Receipts		$520.91

Cash Receipts—NiteGlo Rings		
April 12, 20XX		
Currency		$123.00
Coins		35.84
Checks		45.00
VISA/MC		221.70
Gift Certificates		0.00
Bucks		0.00
Total Receipts		$425.54

Cash Receipts—TurboFlight Tee		
April 12, 20XX		
Currency		$2,170.00
Coins		450.00
Checks		1,527.50
VISA/MC		328.10
Gift Certificates		175.00
Bucks		0.00
Total Receipts		$4,650.60

Cash Receipts—TurboFlight Key		
April 12, 20XX		
Currency		$302.00
Coins		1,754.17
Checks		386.47
VISA/MC		283.15
Gift Certificates		0.00
Bucks		0.00
Total Receipts		$2,725.79

Totals		
Currency		$4,229.00
Coins		2,975.78
Checks		2,835.10
VISA/MC		2,614.82
Gift Certificates		235.00
Bucks		5.00
		$12,894.70
Totals		$12,894.70

In-box 3-1-4

NOTES FROM MELINDA

Create a form to e-mail to reps that requests the following information:

Sales Rep. Name _____

Choice of Days:
1. _____
2. _____
3. _____

Number of Complimentary passes needed:
Adult _____
Child (age 3-7) _____
Senior (over 55) _____
Children under 3 are free

Number of rooms to reserve at the Prism Hotel:
Single (1 double bed) _____
Double (2 double beds) _____
Quad (2 double beds & sleep sofa _____

E-mail return by 4-20

4-14-20xx

Notes 3-2-1

NOTES FROM MELINDA

Reports that should be sent to the sales representatives are:

- *the Group Sales report that displays both a bar chart showing sales by quarter and pie chart that shows sales by category*
- *Group Sales Projections report that shows the spreadsheet and includes a bar chart below the spreadsheet. The bar chart should display each quarter and increase for each quarter. Here is a copy of last year's chart to use as an example. Remember to include the 8% increase for the year.*

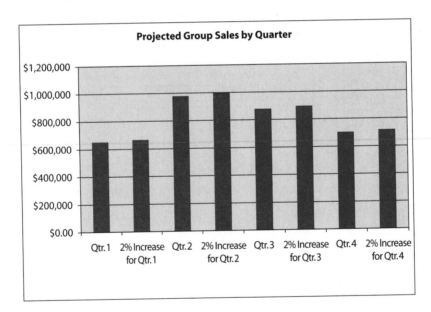

4-14-20xx

Notes 3-2-2

April 20, 20XX

Project 4—Days One through Five Procedures

April 20, 20XX

In order to complete the tasks in this project, you will need to assemble the following information:

- E-mail messages from Melinda O'Neal, your supervisor, found on the student CD.
- *Notes from Melinda,* written messages from Melinda.
- *In-box* items, source documents needed for completing the tasks.
- *To Do* lists, additional notes to self on tasks. In this project, you will also find a To Do from Melinda.

Detailed directions for completing the tasks are in the e-mail messages and *Notes from Melinda.* The *In-box* items are source documents needed to complete tasks. The *To Do* lists give additional notes to self to complete tasks.

1. Open EM 4-20 file from your student CD-ROM. All e-mail messages for the week are dated beginning with 4-20A (April 20) through 4-24 (April 24) and are stored as EM4-20A, EM4-20B, EM4-21, EM4-23, etc. Most e-mail messages are from Melinda O'Neal, your supervisor. Print and read all the messages, however.

2. Next, look at all the In-box forms marked *In-box 4-1-1* that are related to the EM 4-20B e-mail message and the Notes from Melinda labeled *Notes 4-1-1* in the student workbook. EM 4-20B, the second e-mail of 4-20, is an e-mail to you and relates specifically to the Notes marked *Notes 4-1-1* (Project 4, Day 1, Task 1) and *In-box 4-1-1* and *4-1-2* (Project 4, Day 1, Tasks 1 and 2). Day 2 is EM 4-21 and relates specifically to the To Do marked 4-21 and *In-box 4-2-1.*

3. Continue matching e-mail messages with any related Notes and/or In-box documents for the week.

4. Use the Project 4 Worksheet Plan to organize the tasks for the week. Use the Sample Worksheet Plan in the Reference section as a guide. Forms are available on the student CD.

5. As each e-mail task and related source documents are reviewed, enter on the Worksheet Plan the task to be completed, the date required, software to be used, and the estimated time to complete.

6. When the plan is complete, put the forms in a folder labeled *Current Projects.*

7. Use the bottom part of the Plan to prioritize the jobs. List them in the order in which you will complete them. Take into consideration when items need to be used, mailed, distributed, etc.

8. Complete each task in the order of priority you choose. Place the completed documents in a folder marked *Completed Projects* and place the source documents and messages in a folder marked *Stored Documents*.

   Option: Save the files with a file name that identifies the project, the day, and the task number. For example, Task 3 of Project 4 on Day 1 would be saved as p4d1t3. Place all files for Project 4 in a folder named *Project 4*. Repeat this process for all projects. The teacher then has the option of grading documents electronically. Place an electronic copy of the project evaluation in the folder.

9. Any job carried over to the next week (Project 5) should be written at the bottom of the form in the space provided. Incomplete source documents and tasks should be kept in the *Current Projects* folder.

10. Complete the Project Evaluation form provided in the manual and on the student CD for Project 4.

   Repeat this procedure for each day of the week through April 24.

   When all the work for Project 4 is completed, place the Project 4 Worksheet Plan and completed Project Evaluation in the front of the folder marked *Completed Projects* and give the entire folder to your instructor for evaluation.

PROJECT 4 WORKSHEET PLAN

Start Date_____   End Date_____

List Items:	Task	Date Needed	Software Required	Estimated Time Needed
___E-mail	_____	_____	_____	_____
	_____	_____	_____	_____
	_____	_____	_____	_____
	_____	_____	_____	_____
	_____	_____	_____	_____
	_____	_____	_____	_____
	_____	_____	_____	_____
	_____	_____	_____	_____
	_____	_____	_____	_____
	_____	_____	_____	_____
	_____	_____	_____	_____
___Notes from Melinda	_____	_____	_____	_____
	_____	_____	_____	_____
	_____	_____	_____	_____
	_____	_____	_____	_____
___Other Source Documents	_____	_____	_____	_____
	_____	_____	_____	_____
	_____	_____	_____	_____
___Jobs in Progress	_____	_____	_____	_____
	_____	_____	_____	_____

List the jobs to be completed by priority. Check off as completed.

	Task Completed	Completion Time
____	_____	_____
____	_____	_____
____	_____	_____
____	_____	_____
____	_____	_____
____	_____	_____
____	_____	_____
____	_____	_____

On-going tasks to carry over: _____
_____

Project Evaluation

Employee Name _____ **Start Date** _____

Project Number _____ **End Date** _____

Write the number of the task and use check marks to indicate that you have completed the following procedures. In the space provided, identify any problems encountered and how you solved them.

Project # & Task # (1-1-1)	Software Used	Spell Checked	Proofread (Grammar & Punctuation)	Accuracy (Dates, Amounts, & Facts)	Neatness (no smudges, tears, or folds)	Formatting Checked (spacing, margins, etc.)	Problem Encountered	Solution

Other Comments

Suggestions or Recommendations _____

Supervisor's Signature _____ **Project Grade** _____

PROJECT 4

★COASTERS, ETC.★

May 8, 20XX

Attention College Relations Director

COLLEGE NITE *change all occurrences to night*

Coasters, Etc. is happy to present our ~~Second~~ *First* Annual College ~~Nite~~. *Night on June 5* This night has been set aside for an exclusive park party for college students. Each student will be able to buy tickets at a reduced rate of $20, $6 less than the normal price. The park will be closed to the general public between the hours of 5:~~00~~ p.m. and midnight. Students can enjoy ONE big night to themselves~~, and~~ they can meet new friends from other campuses across four states while riding all ~~your~~ *their* favorite rides, listening to a Battle of the Bands, and enjoying great food.

Here's the bonus! For every 15 tickets sold, ~~1~~ *one* free admission ticket is given to the coordinator. The offer is unlimited; if you ~~sold~~ *sell* 150 ticket~~s~~ *s*, you or the club or organization ~~would~~ *will* receive ~~15~~ *10* free tickets.

tr ~~En~~closed are posters and flyers that can be passed~~/~~on to clubs and organizations. *Of course,* The College Relations Department may want to handle the entire promotion. Students must buy tickets in advance by signing up on *the* ~~enclosed forms~~ *sign-up sheets*. Tickets will be mailed to the club or organization coordinator for distribution. For students who already have a Coasters' Season Pass, the cost is only $15 for admission. *when they present their ticket plus their pass at the admission gate.*
Also enclosed *are* several coordinator packets. These include sign-up sheets, order forms, and all the directions for handling COLLEGE NITE. These can be distributed with the posters and flyers.

Don't let your students miss out on a well deserved ~~great~~ night of fun ~~they deserve~~! We ~~sold out last year and~~ expect a sell-out, so please distribute the packets promptly. Orders must be received by May 27. *this year*

We look forward to entertaining your students and their guests.

Sincerely,

Melinda O'Neal, Office Manager
wf ~~Group Sales~~
Enclosures

3000 Prism Highway, Castle Rock, CO 80732
1-800-555-3251
Fax: 1-303-555-1212   http://www.prism.coaster.com   E-mail: coasters@prism.com

In-box 4-1-1

COLLEGE NIGHT—FRIDAY, JUNE 5, 20XX
5 p.m.–Midnight

A 'jammin' night of fun!

For $20 or $15 with a Season Pass look at what you get—

- A great way to celebrate the end of a hectic academic year:

- A meal ticket that may be used in the "Picnic Grove" area, which will be open 6 p.m.–8 p.m. Menu includes hamburger, hotdog, or pizza; chips or fruit; juice or soft drinks; ice cream or yogurt.

- Entertainment by three reggae bands will be featured in the Prism Amphitheater. Join new friends from a 4-state area for a "jammin" night of fun.

- All of your favorite rides, including this year's new special attraction—Devil's Backbone—will be available. This is a bone-chilling coaster ride that has the rider standing and held securely in place as the coaster goes through inversions at backbreaking speed.

Remember last year's major ride, Pit Alley? This race car simulator takes you out on the racing tarmac where speeds and turns and the swerving of an Indy 500 race car drive are simulated. Even the pit stop with a tire change is a thrill.

- The arcade will be open so you can play all your favorite games and win prizes.

- Even your favorite water rides will be running. The Mountain Logger takes you through rapids and tree tops in a hollowed-out log. The Lost River travels through marshes and jungles of an ancient land inhabited by wild creatures and animals; then it ends in a terrifying drop over a 500-foot waterfall. You may get wet so be sure to bring extra clothes!

In-box 4-1-2

NOTES FROM MELINDA

Create a tri-fold flyer for the College Night promotion. See your In-box for the layout of a tri-fold flyer. Use standard 8 ½ x 11 paper in wide orientation. Another chance to be creative!

4/20/20xx

Notes 4-1-1

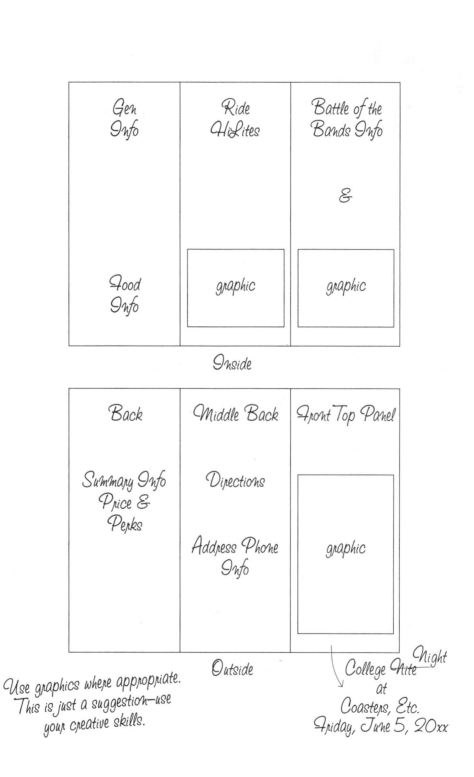

Gen Info	Ride HiLites	Battle of the Bands Info
		&
Food Info	graphic	graphic

Inside

Back	Middle Back	Front Top Panel
Summary Info Price & Perks	Directions	graphic
	Address Phone Info	

Outside

Use graphics where appropriate.
This is just a suggestion—use
your creative skills.

College Nite Night
at
Coasters, Etc.
Friday, June 5, 20xx

In-box 4-1-2

AA—Change all occurrences of Grad Nite to College Night

❒ YES! We want to join the fun of Grad Nite 20XX Friday, June 5. Enclosed is our check payable to Coasters, Etc. (Do not send cash, personal checks, or purchase orders for payment.) One meal ticket is issued with each complimentary ticket.

Name of School _____

Your Name _____

School Phone _____

Name and address where Grad Nite tickets should be mailed:

Name _____

Mailing Address _____

City _____ State _____ Zip _____
20
_____ Grad Nite Tickets (original order must be 15 or more tickets . . . × $22.00 = $_____

_____ Grad Nite Tickets for Season Pass holders . . . . × $15.00 = $_____
You must bring both your 20XX Coasters, Etc. Season Pass and your College Night admission ticket for admission

❒ Please reserve _____ Complimentary coordinator passes.
(One complimentary pass for every 15 tickets sold for Grad Nite.)

Organizers' Names:

_____

_____

_____

*On Grad Nite, pick up FREE tickets for coordinators at the Window marked "Organizer Tickets." Please list their names in the spaces provided.

Use the enclosed envelope and mail this form—along with your payment to: Coasters, Etc. Grad Nite 20XX Dept. 953-CN, 3000 Prism Highway, Castle Rock, CO 80732. The deadline for ticket orders is May 24.
27

For park use only:

Date Rec'd. _____ Confirmation _____ Contacted _____ Check/M.O. No. _____

In-box 4-2-1

Sign Up for Grad Nite

AA–Change all occurrences of Grad Nite to College Night

Keep track of names and payment information for each person attending Grad Nite 20XX. Use this sheet . . . then keep it for your records. Do not return this sheet. If you need extra Sign-Up Sheets, just make copies of this form.

Name	Number of $20 Tickets	Number of $15 Tickets	Amount Due	Amount Paid
_____	_____	_____	_____	_____
_____	_____	_____	_____	_____
_____	_____	_____	_____	_____
_____	_____	_____	_____	_____
_____	_____	_____	_____	_____
_____	_____	_____	_____	_____
_____	_____	_____	_____	_____
_____	_____	_____	_____	_____
_____	_____	_____	_____	_____
_____	_____	_____	_____	_____
_____	_____	_____	_____	_____
_____	_____	_____	_____	_____
_____	_____	_____	_____	_____
TOTAL			_____	_____

Grad Nite requires a special ticket which must be purchased in advance. NO TICKETS WILL BE SOLD AT THE GATE. NO OTHER PRE-SOLD TICKETS (such as Good Any Day Tickets) OR SEASON PASSES without special GRAD NITE tickets will be accepted.

1. Compute the correct amount each person owes and enter in "Amount Due" column.
2. As each person pays what he or she owes, enter that amount in "Amount Paid" column.
3. After everyone has signed up, total the "Amount Due" and "Amount Paid" columns.

In-box 4-2-1

93

To do...

title

Tuesday—gather faxes/e-mails from reps. Set up forecasting meeting and park duty schedules. Avoid conflicts. No Saturdays or Sundays. Use a table to organize the schedule.

Name	Dates Required	Days of Week	Meeting w. S. Chaverez	Park Duty	
				Day 1	Day 2

Send schedule to Sally Chaverez (or her assistant) requesting her to confirm by Thursday, 4/23, and e-mail to you her "OK." Sort the database by last name in ascending order.

After SC confirms, e-mail the hotel and attach the schedule of reps' requested dates and make reservations. Ask the hotel concierge to put together a packet that includes the complimentary park passes and dinner report forms for each rep.

This Week—

Don't forget this weekend's cash receipt tally.
Prepare the roller coaster facts report from information found on the Internet two weeks ago.
Update calendar!

4/21/20xx

Forecasting Meeting &
Park Duty Request

Sales Representative: **David Alcox**

List three 3-day periods in order of preference from May 1 through August 31 for your meeting and park duty assignments:

1. _June 10, 11, 12_   A

2. _June 14, 15, 16_

3. _June 18, 19, 20_

The number of complimentary park admission tickets needed:

_2_   adults

_4_   children (ages 3–7); children under 3 are free

_____   seniors (over 55)

Complimentary room reservations needed:

Single—(1 double bed) ☑

Double—(2 double beds) ☑

Quad—(2 double beds and 1 sleep sofa) ❑

Additional request: _Connecting rooms or a quad_

Your complimentary passes and room reservations are limited to immediate family including spouse, children, and parents.

Dave Alcox

Sales Representative

In-box 4-2-2

Forecasting Meeting &
Park Duty Request

Sales Representative: **Ed Alverez**

List three 3-day periods in order of preference from May 1 through August 31 for your meeting and park duty assignments:

1. _July 5, 6, 7_

2. _July 13, 14, 15_ ✳

3. _July 19, 20, 21_

The number of complimentary park admission tickets needed:

__2__ adults

__3__ children (ages 3–7); children under 3 are free

_____ seniors (over 55)

Complimentary room reservations needed:

Single—(1 double bed) ❏

Double—(2 double beds) ❏

Quad—(2 double beds and 1 sleep sofa) ☑

Additional request: _____

Your complimentary passes and room reservations are limited to immediate family including spouse, children, and parents.

Ed Alverez

Sales Representative

In-box 4-2-2

Forecasting Meeting &
Park Duty Request

Sales Representative: **Rich Hoffman**

List three 3-day periods in order of preference from May 1 through August 31 for your
meeting and park duty assignments:

1. *May 26, 27, 28*

2. *May 21, 22, 23*

3. *June 4, 5, 6*

The number of complimentary park admission tickets needed:

___2___   adults

_____   children (ages 3–7); children under 3 are free

_____   seniors (over 55)

Complimentary room reservations needed:

Single—(1 double bed) ☑

Double—(2 double beds) ❏

Quad—(2 double beds and 1 sleep sofa) ❏

Additional request: _____

Your complimentary passes and room reservations are limited to immediate family
including spouse, children, and parents.

Rich Hoffman

Sales Representative

In-box 4-2-2

Forecasting Meeting &
Park Duty Request

Sales Representative: **Alvin Lujan**

List three 3-day periods in order of preference from May 1 through August 31 for your meeting and park duty assignments:

1. _June 23, 24, 25_

2. _June 25, 26, 27_

3. _June 28, 29, 30_

The number of complimentary park admission tickets needed:

__2__ adults

__5__ children (ages 3–7); children under 3 are free

_____ seniors (over 55)

Complimentary room reservations needed:

Single—(1 double bed) ☑

Double—(2 double beds) ☐

Quad—(2 double beds and 1 sleep sofa) ☑

Additional request: _need connecting rooms_

Your complimentary passes and room reservations are limited to immediate family including spouse, children, and parents.

Alvin Lujan

Sales Representative

In-box 4-2-2

Forecasting Meeting & Park Duty Request

Sales Representative: **Amy Margolies**

List three 3-day periods in order of preference from May 1 through August 31 for your meeting and park duty assignments:

1. _June 18, 19, 20_

2. _June 1, 2, 3_ ✳

3. _July 29, 30, August 1_

The number of complimentary park admission tickets needed:

__1__ adults

_____ children (ages 3–7); children under 3 are free

__2__ seniors (over 55)

Complimentary room reservations needed:

Single—(1 double bed) ☑

Double—(2 double beds) ☐

Quad—(2 double beds and 1 sleep sofa) ☐

Additional request: _need two singles, connecting if possible_

Your complimentary passes and room reservations are limited to immediate family including spouse, children, and parents.

Amy Margolies

Sales Representative

In-box 4-2-2

Forecasting Meeting &
Park Duty Request

Sales Representative: **Dave Mattis**

List three 3-day periods in order of preference from May 1 through August 31 for your meeting and park duty assignments:

1. _June 17, 18, 19_ ★

2. _July 6, 7, 8_

3. _July 29, 30, 31_

The number of complimentary park admission tickets needed:

_2_ adults

_2_ children (ages 3–7); children under 3 are free

_____ seniors (over 55)

Complimentary room reservations needed:

Single—(1 double bed) ❑

Double—(2 double beds) ☑

Quad—(2 double beds and 1 sleep sofa) ❑

Additional request: _____

Your complimentary passes and room reservations are limited to immediate family including spouse, children, and parents.

Dave Mattis

Sales Representative

In-box 4-2-2

Forecasting Meeting &
Park Duty Request

Sales Representative: **T. J. Meier**

List three 3-day periods in order of preference from May 1 through August 31 for your meeting and park duty assignments:

1. *August 5, 6, 7*

2. *August 8, 9, 10*

3. *August 10, 11, 12*

The number of complimentary park admission tickets needed:

__2__ adults

_____ children (ages 3–7); children under 3 are free

_____ seniors (over 55)

Complimentary room reservations needed:

Single—(1 double bed) ☑

Double—(2 double beds) ☐

Quad—(2 double beds and 1 sleep sofa) ☐

Additional request: _____

Your complimentary passes and room reservations are limited to immediate family including spouse, children, and parents.

T. J. Meier

Sales Representative

In-box 4-2-2

PROJECT 4

Forecasting Meeting &
Park Duty Request

Sales Representative: **Ron Patterson**

List three 3-day periods in order of preference from May 1 through August 31 for your meeting and park duty assignments:

1. *May 22, 23, 24*

2. *June 1, 2, 3* ✳

3. *June 4, 5, 6*

The number of complimentary park admission tickets needed:

__1__ adults

_____ children (ages 3–7); children under 3 are free

_____ seniors (over 55)

Complimentary room reservations needed:

Single—(1 double bed) ☑

Double—(2 double beds) ☐

Quad—(2 double beds and 1 sleep sofa) ☐

Additional request: _____

Your complimentary passes and room reservations are limited to immediate family including spouse, children, and parents.

Ron Patterson

Sales Representative

In-box 4-2-2

Forecasting Meeting & Park Duty Request

Sales Representative: **George Schwarz**

List three 3-day periods in order of preference from May 1 through August 31 for your meeting and park duty assignments:

1. *June 8, 9, 10* ✳

2. *June 10, 11, 12*

3. *May 23, 24, 25*

The number of complimentary park admission tickets needed:

__2__ adults

__2__ children (ages 3–7); children under 3 are free

_____ seniors (over 55)

Complimentary room reservations needed:

Single—(1 double bed) ❏

Double—(2 double beds) ☑

Quad—(2 double beds and 1 sleep sofa) ❏

Additional request: _____

Your complimentary passes and room reservations are limited to immediate family including spouse, children, and parents.

George Schwarz

Sales Representative

In-box 4-2-2

NOTES FROM MELINDA

After the forecasting schedule has been confirmed by S. Chaverez, e-mail the schedule to the reps so they will know the dates of their park visit and meeting. Ask them to be prepared for their forecasting meeting by bringing with them the following:

- Forecast Planning Report for next year
- Monthly activity sheets from last year-to-date
- Summary of 2-week itinerary forms
- Group Sales Analysis Report

Let the reps know that reservations have been made at the hotel as they requested. Breakfast is complimentary for all registered hotel guests. Lunch is on their own, but dinner is complimentary for all reps and their families if they sign the dinner receipt forms which will be in their hotel packets when they register.

4-23-20xx

Notes 4-4-1

Coasters, Etc. Group Sales

Quarterly Call Report

Name: _Dave Alcox_   **Qtr. Ending** _March 31_

Date	Company Name/Address	Contact Person	Type of Call — Company	Organization	School	Other	Reason for Call — Sale	Follow Up	Service	Other	Results/Comments FT/PT # of Employees
20XX Jan. 5	Colorado Electric Company–North 9503 N. 35th Street Fort Collins, CO 81520-9393 1-970-555-9948	Julia Margolies	x				x				325
Jan. 5	Rocky Mountain West Airlines 5422 Airport Road Boulder, CO 81530-4393 1-970-555-1121	John Kovach	x					x			150
Jan. 12	Sky West Airlines 5430 Airport Road Boulder, CO 81530-4393 1-970-555-3934	Ben Rubin	x				x				95
Jan. 18	Mile High Hotels/Motels–N. CO 12 Ski Mountain Pass Aspen, CO 81650-2001 1-970-555-1000	Elaine Hollis	x				x				415
Feb. 3	Mountain Loggers Inc. 25 Aspen Highway Steamboat Springs, CO 81835-3990 1-970-555-4560	Larry Marshall	x					x			75
Mar. 3	Northern Colorado Hospital Alliance 1500 N. High Street Boulder, CO 81530-9900 1-970-555-9900	James Hosty, Administrative Director									550

Additional Comments   _all new B & I contracts_

Distribution: **White:** –Sales Manager   **Canary:** –Group Sales Office   **Pink:** –Retain

In-box 4-5-1

Coasters, Etc. Group Sales

Quarterly Call Report

Name: _Ed Alvarez_   Qtr. Ending _March 31_

Date	Company Name/Address	Contact Person	Type of Call — Company	Organization	School	Other	Reason for Call — Sale	Follow Up	Service	Other	Results/Comments FT/PT # of Employees
20XX Jan. 27	Talledega Resort P.O. Box 57 Durango, CO 82080-2931 1-970-555-0989	Jessey Zilch	x				x			* _Resort program_	325/1000 _guest capacity_
Feb. 5	West CO Honda Assembly Plant 3000 Continental Divide Highway Grand Junction, CO 81930-3933 1-970-555-1234	Imko Ohasa	x					x			625
Feb. 8	Montrose Lumber Co. 700 Highlands Blvd. Montrose, CO 81930-3923 1-970-555-3960	Judy Hamilton	x				x				150
Feb. 15	Western State College–Employee Relations 3000 Campus Highway Gunnison, CO 82030-4526 1-970-555-2112	Raymond Smith	x				x				450
Feb. 26	Ski Sunlight Resort 900 Cattle Creek Glenwood Springs, CO 82030-4522 1-970-555-4044	Charlene Robinson	x					x		_Resort program_	200/750 _guest capacity_
Mar. 15	Telluride Ski Resort 790 Sawpit Road Telluride, CO 81909-6553 1-970-555-7930	Cassidy Griffin								_Resort program_	275/1000 _guest capacity_

Additional Comments _sold * resort program—discount tickets for all guests of the resort._

Distribution: **White:** –Sales Manager   **Canary:** –Group Sales Office   **Pink:** –Retain

In-box 4-5-1

Coasters, Etc. Group Sales

Quarterly Call Report

Name: T. J. Meier

Qtr. Ending March 31

| Date | Company Name/Address | Contact Person | Type of Call | | | | | Reason for Call | | | Results/Comments FT/PT # of Employees |
			Company	Organization	School	Other	Sale	Follow Up	Service	Other	
20XX Jan. 9	US West Communications 500 W. Meridian Ave. Denver, CO 80598-9003 1-303-555-9211	Jane Hoffman	x					x			1250
Jan. 15	Hillenbrande Industries 300 Alameda Ave. Denver, CO 80570-3203 1-303-555-0012	Kevin Kelley, V.P. of Human Resources	x					x			450
Feb. 18	SouthWest Plaza Employee Assoc. 290 W. Bellview Highway Littleton, CO 80730-1102 1-303-555-9393	Madeline Williams, Dir. Mall Employees	x					x			675
Feb. 25	University of Denver–Employee Assoc. 2500 Evans Avenue Denver, CO 80571-7766 1-303-555-5694	Robert Mann, Director	x					x			3250
Mar. 9	Colorado State Government Employees Human Resources–Capitol Building 11 S. Mint Denver, CO 80570-6900 1-303-555-7303	Michael Cross, Director	x					x			2500

Additional Comments

Distribution: **White:** –Sales Manager **Canary:** –Group Sales Office **Pink:** –Retain

In-box 4-5-1

NOTES FROM MELINDA

Attached is a database form to use as a guide when setting up the necessary fields in the B & I database.

4-24-20xx

Notes 4-5-2

Business & Industry

Company Name: Colorado Electric Co.–North   Contact: Julia Margolies

Address: 9503 N. 35th Street
City: Fort Collins   State: CO   Zip: 81520-9393

Phone: 1-970-555-9948   No. Employed: 325
                                                     Resort Program:

Coasters Rep.:   Dave Alcox

In-box 4-5-1

★ COASTERS, ETC. ★

Miscellaneous Cash Receipts Envelope

SIGNATURES

DEPARTMENT: _____
RECEIVED BY: _____

Miscellaneous Cash Receipts

Date _4-19-20xx_

ACCOUNT TO CREDIT	DESCRIPTION		AMOUNT
Key Photos	Promo Sales	500	1893.71
Cotton Candy	Food Sales	600	879.93
Lemon Ice	Food Sales	610	494.73 → ~~175.00~~
Belgian Waffles	Food Sales	650	1472.37
Ice Cream	Food Sales	620	280.00
Balloons	Promo Sales	530	528.45
NiteGlo Rings	Promo Sales	570	730.06
TurboFlight Tee	Promo Sales	510	5693.39
TurboFlight Key	Promo Sales	515	1769.12
		Total	13,741.87

UNIT	CURRENCY
$100	900.00
50	1650.00
20	1100.00
10	870.00
5	580.00
2	14.00
1	375.00
TOTAL	5489.00

UNIT	COIN
$1.00	274.00
.50	250.50
.25	425.25
.10	521.10
.05	375.25
.01	225.15
ROLL COIN	25.00
TOTAL	2096.32

TOTAL CURRENCY $	5489.00
TOTAL COIN $	2096.32 ~~2095.32~~
TOTAL CHECKS $	2925.57
VISA/MC $	2910.94
GIFT CERTIFICATES $	255.00
SCREAMIN' BUCKS $	65.00
_____ $	
_____ $	
TOTAL $	13741.83 ~~13740.83~~

For auditor's use only:

Debits: $ ~~13740.83~~
13741.83

Credits: $ _13741.76_

.07
Over (short): $ ~~.43~~

Auditor:

Please verify all information

In-box 4-5-2

Distribution Summary

Cash Receipts—Key Photos		
April 19, 20XX		
Currency		$550.00
Coins		230.39
Checks		395.00
VISA/MC		698.32
Gift Certificates		15.00
Bucks		5.00
Total Receipts		$1,893.71

Cash Receipts—Cotton Candy		
April 19, 20XX		
Currency		$400.00
Coins		273.50
Checks		75.93
VISA/MC		125.50
Gift Certificates		5.00
Bucks		0.00
Total Receipts		$879.93

Cash Receipts—Lemon Ice		
April 19, 20XX		
Currency		$175.00
Coins		95.93
Checks		39.50
VISA/MC		164.30
Gift Certificates		15.00
Bucks		5.00
Total Receipts		$494.73

Cash Receipts—Ice Cream		
April 19, 20XX		
Currency		$139.00
Coins		75.00
Checks		25.05
VISA/MC		30.95
Gift Certificates		5.00
Bucks		5.00
Total Receipts		$280.00

Cash Receipts—Belgian Waffles		
April 19, 20XX		
Currency		$325.00
Coins		75.90
Checks		295.97
VISA/MC		750.50
Gift Certificates		15.00
Bucks		10.00
Total Receipts		$1,472.37

Cash Receipts—Balloons		
April 19, 20XX		
Currency		$175.00
Coins		203.50
Checks		89.00
VISA/MC		45.95
Gift Certificates		10.00
Bucks		5.00
Total Receipts		$528.45

Cash Receipts—NiteGlo Rings		
April 19, 20XX		
Currency		$105.00
Coins		395.03
Checks		35.03
VISA/MC		175.00
Gift Certificates		15.00
Bucks		5.00
Total Receipts		$730.06

Cash Receipts—TurboFlight Tee		
April 19, 20XX		
Currency		$2,795.00
Coins		450.00
Checks		1,695.00
VISA/MC		578.39
Gift Certificates		150.00
Bucks		25.00
Total Receipts		$5,693.39

Cash Receipts—TurboFlight Key		
April 19, 20XX		
Currency		$825.00
Coins		297.00
Checks		275.09
VISA/MC		342.03
Gift Certificates		25.00
Bucks		5.00
Total Receipts		$1,769.12

Totals		
Currency		$5,489.00
Coins		2,096.25
Checks		2,925.57
VISA/MC		2,910.94
Gift Certificates		255.00
Bucks		65.00
		$13,741.76
Totals		$13,741.76

April 27, 20XX

Project 5—Days One through Five Procedures

April 27, 20XX

In order to complete the tasks in this project, you will need to assemble the following information:

- E-mail messages from Melinda O'Neal, your supervisor, found on the student CD.
- *Notes from Melinda,* written messages from Melinda.
- *In-box* items, source documents needed for completing the tasks.
- *To Do* lists, additional notes to self on tasks.

Detailed directions for completing the tasks are in the e-mail messages and *Notes from Melinda.* The *In-box* items are source documents needed to complete tasks. The *To Do* lists give additional notes to self to complete tasks.

1. Open EM4-27 file from your student CD-ROM. All e-mail messages from the week are dated beginning with 4-27 (April 27) through EM4-28 (April 28) and are stored as EM4-27 and EM4-28. These e-mail messages are from Melinda O'Neal, your supervisor. Print and read the messages.

2. Next, look at all the In-box forms marked *In-box 5-1-1, 5-1-2, 5-1-3,* etc. that are related to the EM 4-27 e-mail message. EM 4-28, the second e-mail is an e-mail to you and there are no related Notes from Melinda or In-box items.

3. Continue matching e-mail messages with any related Notes and/or In-box documents for the week.

4. Use the Project 5 Worksheet Plan to organize the tasks for the week. Use the Sample Worksheet Plan in the Reference section as a guide. Forms are available on the student CD.

5. As each e-mail task and related source documents are reviewed, enter on the Worksheet Plan the task to be completed, the date required, software to be used, and the estimated time to complete.

6. When the plan is complete, put the forms in a folder labeled *Current Projects.*

7. Use the bottom part of the Plan to prioritize the jobs. List them in the order you will complete them. Take into consideration when items need to be used, mailed, distributed, etc.

8. Complete each task as directed in the order of priority you choose. Place the completed documents in a folder marked *Completed Projects* and place the source documents and messages in a folder marked *Stored Documents*.

   Option: Save the files with a file name that identifies the project, the day and the task number. For example, task 3 of Project 5 on day 1 would be saved as p5d1t3. Place all files for Project 5 in a folder named *Project 5*. Repeat this process for all projects. The teacher then has the option of grading documents electronically. Place an electronic copy of the project evaluation in the folder.

9. Any job carried over to the next week should be written at the bottom of the form in the space provided. Incomplete source documents and tasks should be kept in the *Current Projects* folder.

10. Complete the Project Evaluation form provided in the manual and on the student CD for Project 5.

   Repeat this procedure for each day of the week through May 1.

   When all the work for Project 5 is completed, place the Project 5 Worksheet Plan and completed Project Evaluation in the front of the folder marked *Completed Projects* and give the entire folder to your instructor for evaluation.

PROJECT 5 WORKSHEET PLAN

Start Date_____   End Date_____

List Items:	Task	Date Needed	Software Required	Estimated Time Needed
___E-mail	_____	_____	_____	_____
	_____	_____	_____	_____
	_____	_____	_____	_____
	_____	_____	_____	_____
	_____	_____	_____	_____
	_____	_____	_____	_____
	_____	_____	_____	_____
	_____	_____	_____	_____
	_____	_____	_____	_____
	_____	_____	_____	_____
___Notes from Melinda				
	_____	_____	_____	_____
	_____	_____	_____	_____
	_____	_____	_____	_____
	_____	_____	_____	_____
___Other Source Documents				
	_____	_____	_____	_____
	_____	_____	_____	_____
	_____	_____	_____	_____
___Jobs in Progress				
	_____	_____	_____	_____
	_____	_____	_____	_____

List the jobs to be completed by priority. Check off as completed.

	Task Completed	Completion Time
____	_____	_____
____	_____	_____
____	_____	_____
____	_____	_____
____	_____	_____
____	_____	_____
____	_____	_____
____	_____	_____
____	_____	_____

On-going tasks to carry over: _____
_____

Project Evaluation

Employee Name _____

Start Date _____

End Date _____

Project Number _____

Write the number of the task and use check marks to indicate that you have completed the following procedures. In the space provided, identify any problems encountered and how you solved them.

Project # & Task # (1-1-1)	Software Used	Spell Checked	Proofread (Grammar & Punctuation)	Accuracy (Dates, Amounts, & Facts)	Neatness (no smudges, tears, or folds)	Formatting Checked (spacing, margins, etc.)	Problem Encountered	Solution

Other Comments

Suggestions or Recommendations _____

Supervisor's Signature _____ **Project Grade** _____

April 27, 20XX

A.A.–
Use letterhead

<<Company Name>>
<<Contact>>
<<Address>>
<<City>> <<State>> <<Zip>>

<<Company Name>> Days at Coasters, Etc.:

employees

Thank you for your interest in providing Coasters, Etc. admission tickets to your ~~company~~. We are happy to provide you with discounted tickets at the following prices:

Adult (Ages 8–59)	$16.00
Child (Ages 3–7 or 48" and Under)	$12.95
Seniors (Ages 60+)	$12.95

Our General Admission price for Adults is $29—you save $13; and our child/Senior price is $16.95—you save $4. What a great opportunity for your company employees and guests to participate at a great savings.

The following guidelines apply to these discounted tickets:

• The tickets must be pre-paid with your company's check. No personal checks are accepted. Coasters, Etc will process your ticket order after receipt of your payment.
• These tickets are non-refundable and non-returnable. Be sure to order only the amount you need.
• Please allow two weeks for ticket processing and mailing. No "rush" orders are accepted.
• Because of the time and personnel necessary to process and print these special discount tickets, this offer is limited to a one-time order only per season.

A.A.–
Bold as indicated

If you wish to place an order for these tickets, please sign the form below to indicate your agreement with the above guidelines. Make a copy for your records and return the signed form along with your check for the number of tickets desired to:

Coasters, Etc.
Attention: Melinda O'Neal
3000 Prism Highway
Castle Rock, CO 80732

A.A.–
Don't forget the new ¶
from 4-27 e-mail

Thank you again for your interest in Coasters, Etc. We look forward to entertaining you and your guests this exciting season.

Sincerely,

Melinda O'Neal, Division Manager
Group Sales

_____

We understand the guidelines for purchasing discounted tickets for <<Company Name>> Days at Coasters, Etc. We understand that discounted tickets are non-refundable and non-returnable and that this offer is limited to one offer per company per season.

AGREEMENT:

_____   _____
Name   Company Name

In-box 5-1-1

Family Picnic Budget Planner Guide
Example

Country Fried Chicken Dinner

Use right align or decimal tab

All you care to eat

			5.25	
		8.00 ⟵		
Adult	100 @	~~$7.25~~	$725.00	
Child/Senior	10 @	~~4.95~~	495.00	
Subtotal			$2,999.50	
6% tax (food only)			73.20	*recalculate*
Grand Total			**$3,072.70**	

Less Employee Contribution (optional)
$5/per person/110 guests   (500.00)
Company Budget   **$2,522.70**

double-check all figures

> • Estimates based on group size of 110
> • Minimum requirement: 100 adult meals
> • No deposit, no hidden costs!

In-box 5-1-2

★ COASTERS, ETC. ★

Miscellaneous Cash Receipts

Miscellaneous Cash Receipts Envelope

SIGNATURES

DEPARTMENT: _____
RECEIVED BY: _____

Date _4-26-20xx_

ACCOUNT TO CREDIT	DESCRIPTION		AMOUNT
Key Photos	Promo Sales	500	2291.30
Cotton Candy	Food Sales	600	1431.88
Balloons	Promo Sales	530	800.89
NiteGlo Rings	Promo Sales	570	1146.42
Ice Cream	Food Sales	620	1231.00
Lemon Ice	Food Sales	610	1231.37
Turbo Flight Tee	Promo Sales	510	10150.99
Turbo Flight Key	Promo Sales	515	2920.08
Belgian Waffles	Food Sales	650	2048.93

(Total)

UNIT	CURRENCY		UNIT	COIN
$100	3800.00		$1.00	1873.00
50	2500.00		.50	425.00
20	2160.00		.25	575.25
10	1490.00		.10	303.90
5	215.00		.05	80.00
2	6.00		.01	7.39 ~~6.56~~
1	59.00		ROLL COIN	_____
TOTAL	_____		TOTAL	_____

TOTAL CURRENCY	$10,230.00
TOTAL COIN	$3,264.54
TOTAL CHECKS	$4,791.33
VISA/MC	$4,288.99
GIFT CERTIFICATES	$482.00
SCREAMIN' BUCKS	$196.00
_____	$_____
_____	$_____
TOTAL	$_____

For auditor's use only:

Auditor: _____

Debits: $_____   Credits: $_____   Over (short): $_____

A.A.—Total and verify today's receipts and complete this form.

In-box 5-1-3

A.A.—Be sure to verify.

Distribution Summary

Cash Receipts—Key Photos		
April 26, 20XX		
Currency		$789.00
Coins		302.30
Checks		425.00
VISA/MC		725.00
Gift Certificates		30.00
Bucks		20.00
Total Receipts		$2,291.30

Cash Receipts—Cotton Candy		
April 26, 20XX		
Currency		$493.00
Coins		340.50
Checks		212.00
VISA/MC		329.38
Gift Certificates		32.00
Bucks		25.00
Total Receipts		$1,431.88

Cash Receipts—Lemon Ice		
April 26, 20XX		
Currency		$345.00
Coins		230.42
Checks		235.00
VISA/MC		350.95
Gift Certificates		45.00
Bucks		25.00
Total Receipts		$1,231.37

Cash Receipts—Ice Cream		
April 26, 20XX		
Currency		$429.00
Coins		230.00
Checks		130.00
VISA/MC		392.00
Gift Certificates		30.00
Bucks		20.00
Total Receipts		$1,231.00

Cash Receipts—Belgian Waffles		
April 26, 20XX		
Currency		$509.00
Coins		234.93
Checks		439.00
VISA/MC		820.00
Gift Certificates		25.00
Bucks		21.00
Total Receipts		$2,048.93

Cash Receipts—Balloons		
April 26, 20XX		
Currency		$320.00
Coins		245.39
Checks		120.50
VISA/MC		75.00
Gift Certificates		25.00
Bucks		15.00
Total Receipts		$800.89

Cash Receipts—NiteGlo Rings		
April 26, 20XX		
Currency		$305.00
Coins		525.97
Checks		70.50
VISA/MC		204.95
Gift Certificates		25.00
Bucks		15.00
Total Receipts		$1,146.42

Cash Receipts—TurboFlight Tee		
April 26, 20XX		
Currency		$5,790.00
Coins		730.00
Checks		2,505.03
VISA/MC		870.96
Gift Certificates		225.00
Bucks		30.00
Total Receipts		$10,150.99

Cash Receipts—TurboFlight Key		
April 26, 20XX		
Currency		$1,250.00
Coins		425.03
Checks		654.30
VISA/MC		520.75
Gift Certificates		45.00
Bucks		25.00
Total Receipts		$2,920.08

Totals		
Currency		$10,230.03
Coins		3,264.57
Checks		4,791.33
VISA/MC		4,288.99
Gift Certificates		482.00
Bucks		196.00
		$23,252.85
Totals		$23,252.86

PROJECT 5

SAFETY AT COASTERS, ETC.

COASTERS' Safety Philosophy—Providing a safe experience for our guests and ourselves is the most important thing we do.

General First Aid Information

First Aid station is open from 8 a.m. until the last tram has been emptied of guests (about 1 hour after the park has closed).

After hours procedure—call 911, describe injury and report incident to First Aid the next day.

No prescription drugs are available at the First Aid stations. Only aspirin and anti-motion sickness tablets are available for guests and employees.

Facilities are available for guests to store medications.

Your personal Medical Record must be filled out completely and on file when you are processed for employment.

Reporting Injuries

All injured guests and associates should be seen by First Aid. Even minor injuries need to be reported.

Following Safety Procedures—you will be trained on use of equipment, guidelines for safe driving, and proper conduct. Reckless driving and horseplay are grounds for immediate dismissal.

Emergency Assistance

Follow precise procedures in all work locations, including offices.

Minor Accidents/Illness
   If you have any doubt as to the seriousness of an injury or illness, call 911; otherwise follow this procedure:

   1. Direct guest/associate to the First Aid station; take them personally if possible, after receiving permission from your supervisor. If supervisor is unavailable, call 911.
   2. Do not administer First Aid to the person.
   3. Notify your supervisor immediately whenever any incident occurs.

Safety Procedures   Page 1   May 8, 20XX

In-box 5-1-4

Emergencies

(Accidents, illnesses, fires, or need of Police assistance are categorized as emergencies.) Please follow this procedure:

1. Call emergency phone number—EXTENSION 911

   Report to the dispatcher:
     Location and description of patient condition
     Be clear and concise
     In case of fire—describe type (grease, wood, electrical)
     Attempt control of fire with available fire extinguishers

2. Notify your supervisor immediately after calling 911

3. Stay with patient—make as comfortable as possible
   DO NOT attempt to move the patient
   AVOID CONTACT with patient's blood or other bodily fluids

4. Remain calm and try to keep other guests and associates calm in the immediate area.

5. Make no statements regarding insurance, liability, or cause or nature of emergency to anyone. This information must be handled by an authorized individual.

Safety Equipment

Safety equipment includes protective gloves, safety glasses, protective shoes, proper ladders, and carts for carrying equipment. Always use appropriate safety equipment for the situation.

First Care Kits

First Care Kits are located at all work stations and contain supplies needed for initial response to an injury. Supplies include gauze, scissors, tape, and Band-Aids of various sizes. In addition, each box contains personal protective equipment to be used by any of the following:

* First Aid and Security personnel responding to a call
* A companion who is with an injured guest
* Anyone assisting an injured guest

Safety Procedures   Page 2   May 8, 20XX

In-box 5-1-4

Associates use First Care Kit supplies to ensure proper protection against direct contact with bodily fluids and bodily wastes. Any associate who does come into direct contact with blood or bodily fluids MUST report the contact to First Aid immediately.

* Also included in the First Care Kit is a biohazard bag for soiled garments that come into contact with blood or bodily fluids. Soiled garments must be placed in the bag prior to turning into Wardrobe in order to properly alert our Wardrobe personnel.

Sun Protection

Protect yourself from the dangerous effects of too much sun. Avoid prematurely aged skin and skin cancer. Use SPF #15 or higher sunscreen. Protect your eyes from damaging ultraviolet rays; wear sunglasses that provide 100% UV protection. Your park discount applies to sun protection products and sunglasses.

Fires

Fire extinguishers are located throughout the park in all buildings and near all rides. You will be trained in the proper handling of this equipment. Notify your supervisor whenever an extinguisher is used so it can be refilled or replaced. Removing fire extinguishers from their locations or using them for any purpose other than fires may result in immediate termination of employees.

Any fire hazard or safety problem should be reported immediately to your supervisor or the Fire and Safety Department.

Your Right to Know

During your course of employment, you may come in contact, either directly or indirectly, with chemicals and other various materials. You should be familiar with your department's written hazard communications program, a list of chemicals and materials used in your area, and correct use of Material Safety Data Sheets. Your supervisor is responsible for your training in the use of these chemicals and materials and for an explanation of the Right-to-Know policy.

Park Police Assistance

Call Extension 911 any time you encounter or witness an unruly guest, a situation that may require the attention of a Security Officer. Relay the location and all pertinent details.

Take no action yourself.

It is extremely important that all violations be handled by properly trained personnel.

Safety Procedures   Page 3   May 8, 20XX

In-box 5-1-4

NOTES FROM MELINDA

1. Will you do an Internet search for the latest coaster promotions at amusement parks in areas around Prism Parks? Include both wooden and steel. See the map indicating all Prism Park locations.

2. I need the detailed info on this year's AIMS conference if available. Earlier this month you gave me some basic information. I would like to know what sessions they are offering and any details that might now be available. Also refresh my memory on the basic who, where, what, and cost, etc.

3. Set up the Conference Room for the May 1 Marketing Division meeting from 3 to 5 p.m. (send Jeannie Ryan a memo). Send a memo to Linda Day to order refreshments to be delivered to the Conference Room by 2:45 p.m.

4-28-20xx

Notes 5-2-1

Memo

★ COASTERS, ETC.★

TO: Administrative Assistant

FROM: Melinda

DATE: April 28, 20XX

SUBJECT: INCOMING MATH & SCIENCE ORDERS

Attached is a table showing the incoming ticket, food, and material orders from area schools. Mike Anthony, Math & Science Day coordinator, compiled the information from the order forms. Please set up spreadsheets to include all the pertinent information regarding tickets, food, and materials ordered. We should be able to see at a glance the necessary information for each school.

Put ticket and food orders on one spreadsheet and the book materials on another. Be sure to include totals on each spreadsheet. Include an Amount Paid column to show the total materials ordered and the amount received.

By using spreadsheets, we can easily add incoming orders and have continuously updated figures.

xx

In-box 5-2-2

Memo

TO: Melinda O'Neal

FROM: Mike Anthony

DATE: April 21, 20XX

SUBJECT: INCOMING MATH & SCIENCE ORDERS

Below are two tables that I compiled from the first order forms for Math & Science Day tickets, food, and materials. This list should probably be set up in a spreadsheet format so we can view day-to-day increases. There is no charge for Season Pass holders, but they need to present a Math & Science Day worksheet at the gate.

Tickets and Food Orders

School Teacher	Number of Paid Tickets			Comp. Tick. (NC)	Season Pass (NC)	Meal Ticket Order $4.50 each	Amount Paid	Amount Owed or (overpaid)
	Student $16	Child/Senior $12.95	Adult $16					
Alamosa H.S. Juanita Sanchez	65	0	3	4	0	72	1412.00	0
Manitou High School Jane Hoffman	125	0	5	8	20	158	2791.00	0
Kennedy Jr. High School Randy Corgan	75	0	0	5	10	80	1560.00	0
Durango High School Elizabeth Margulies	45	0	2	3	0	50	977.00	0
Mt. Notre Dame High School Salli Sherman	95	0	3	6	0	104	2036.00	0
Moeller High School Ron Hafer	225	0	10	15	30	280	5020.00	0

Materials Booklets

School Teacher	Middle Math	High School Math	General Science (K–8)	Physics (9–12)	Biology (9–12)	All Sciences (9–12)
Alamosa H.S. Juanita Sanchez		1		1	1	
Manitou High School Jane Hoffman		1		1	1	
Kennedy Jr. High School Randy Corgan	1		1			
Durango High School Elizabeth Margulies		1		1		
Mt. Notre Dame High School Salli Sherman				1	1	
Moeller High School Ron Hafer				1	1	

*All material booklets are $5 each.

PROJECT 5

NOTES FROM MELINDA

Go ahead and run the B & I merge for the companies listed in your database. We will add the others when the reps send them to me.

Use the letter created from draft earlier this week and be sure to use the letterhead template you created earlier this month. Don't forget the second page heading.

Melinda

4-29-20xx

Notes 5-3-1

To do...

This Week

–20xx

To do...

_____

This Week

−20xx

To do...

This Week

–20xx

To do...

This Week

−20xx

To do...

This Week

–20xx

★ COASTERS, ETC. ★

Miscellaneous Cash Receipts Envelope

SIGNATURES

DEPARTMENT: _____
RECEIVED BY: _____

Miscellaneous Cash Receipts

Date _____

ACCOUNT TO CREDIT	DESCRIPTION	AMOUNT

UNIT	CURRENCY
$100	_____
50	_____
20	_____
10	_____
5	_____
2	_____
1	_____
TOTAL	_____

UNIT	COIN
$1.00	_____
.50	_____
.25	_____
.10	_____
.05	_____
.01	_____
ROLL COIN	_____
TOTAL	_____

TOTAL CURRENCY	$	_____
TOTAL COIN	$	_____
TOTAL CHECKS	$	_____
VISA/MC	$	_____
GIFT CERTIFICATES	$	_____
SCREAMIN' BUCKS	$	_____
_____	$	_____
_____	$	_____
TOTAL	$	_____

For auditor's use only:

Auditor: _____

Debits: $_____   Credits: $_____   Over (short): $_____

★ COASTERS, ETC.★

Miscellaneous Cash Receipts

Miscellaneous Cash Receipts
Envelope

SIGNATURES

DEPARTMENT: _____
RECEIVED BY: _____

Date _____

ACCOUNT TO CREDIT	DESCRIPTION	AMOUNT

UNIT	CURRENCY	UNIT	COIN		
$100	_____	$1.00	_____	TOTAL CURRENCY	$_____
50	_____	.50	_____	TOTAL COIN	$_____
20	_____	.25	_____	TOTAL CHECKS	$_____
10	_____	.10	_____	VISA/MC	$_____
5	_____	.05	_____	GIFT CERTIFICATES	$_____
2	_____	.01	_____	SCREAMIN' BUCKS	$_____
1	_____	ROLL COIN	_____	_____	$_____
TOTAL	_____	TOTAL	_____	_____	$_____
				TOTAL	$_____

For auditor's use only: Auditor:

Debits: $_____   Credits: $_____   Over (short): $_____

★ COASTERS, ETC. ★

Miscellaneous Cash Receipts

Miscellaneous Cash Receipts Envelope

SIGNATURES

DEPARTMENT: _____
RECEIVED BY: _____

Date _____

ACCOUNT TO CREDIT	DESCRIPTION	AMOUNT

UNIT	CURRENCY		UNIT	COIN			
$100	_____		$1.00	_____	TOTAL CURRENCY	$	_____
50	_____		.50	_____	TOTAL COIN	$	_____
20	_____		.25	_____	TOTAL CHECKS	$	_____
10	_____		.10	_____	VISA/MC	$	_____
5	_____		.05	_____	GIFT CERTIFICATES	$	_____
2	_____		.01	_____	SCREAMIN' BUCKS	$	_____
1	_____		ROLL COIN	_____	_____	$	_____
TOTAL	_____		TOTAL	_____	_____	$	_____
					TOTAL	$	_____

For auditor's use only: Auditor: _____

Debits: $_____   Credits: $_____   Over (short): $_____

Miscellaneous Cash Receipts Envelope

SIGNATURES

DEPARTMENT: _____
RECEIVED BY: _____

Miscellaneous Cash Receipts

Date _____

ACCOUNT TO CREDIT	DESCRIPTION	AMOUNT

UNIT	CURRENCY	UNIT	COIN		
$100	_____	$1.00	_____	TOTAL CURRENCY	$_____
50	_____	.50	_____	TOTAL COIN	$_____
20	_____	.25	_____	TOTAL CHECKS	$_____
10	_____	.10	_____	VISA/MC	$_____
5	_____	.05	_____	GIFT CERTIFICATES	$_____
2	_____	.01	_____	SCREAMIN' BUCKS	$_____
1	_____	ROLL COIN	_____	_____	$_____
TOTAL	_____	TOTAL	_____	_____	$_____
				TOTAL	$_____

For auditor's use only: Auditor:

Debits: $_____   Credits: $_____   Over (short): $_____

★ COASTERS, ETC. ★

Miscellaneous Cash Receipts Envelope

SIGNATURES

DEPARTMENT: _____
RECEIVED BY: _____

Miscellaneous Cash Receipts

Date _____

ACCOUNT TO CREDIT	DESCRIPTION	AMOUNT

UNIT	CURRENCY	UNIT	COIN		
$100	_____	$1.00	_____	TOTAL CURRENCY	$_____
50	_____	.50	_____	TOTAL COIN	$_____
20	_____	.25	_____	TOTAL CHECKS	$_____
10	_____	.10	_____	VISA/MC	$_____
5	_____	.05	_____	GIFT CERTIFICATES	$_____
2	_____	.01	_____	SCREAMIN' BUCKS	$_____
1	_____	ROLL COIN	_____	_____	$_____
TOTAL	_____	TOTAL	_____	_____	$_____
				TOTAL	$_____

For auditor's use only: Auditor:

Debits: $_____   Credits: $_____   Over (short): $_____